INSPIRING STORIES OF 21ST CENTURY SOCCER STARS FOR KIDS

DISCOVER THE AMAZING JOURNEYS, POWERFUL
LESSONS, AND SECRET SUCCESS FORMULA
OF MODERN SOCCER CHAMPIONS
FOR YOUNG FANS AND ASPIRING PLAYERS

AXEL LARKSON

Disclaimer Notice:
This book is a creative retelling of the lives and achievements of various soccer athletes. While it is inspired by real events and personalities, it should be noted that some elements have been fictionalized for narrative enhancement. The dialogues, scenarios, and certain events have been crafted for storytelling purposes and may not accurately represent historical facts or the precise words spoken by the athletes.

The images included in this book are artistic representations and are intended for illustrative purposes only. They are not actual photographs of the athletes during competitions, nor are they meant to depict the exact likeness of any individual. No endorsement by or affiliation with any person depicted is intended or should be inferred.

Readers are encouraged to consult additional sources if they seek factual accounts of the athletes' lives and careers. This book aims to inspire and entertain by celebrating the spirit and achievements of women in sports through a blend of fact and fiction.

Table of Contents

Your Feedback is Treasured!

I love hearing what you and your kids think!

Once you've turned the last page, please take a moment to leave a honest review.

Sharing your insights can make a big difference!

It helps other families find this book and enjoy the stories as much as you did.

Let's spread the joy and inspiration together!

INTRODUCTION

What do all great soccer champions have in common? Is there a secret formula they can teach us? What makes Lionel Messi, Cristiano Ronaldo, Carli Lloyd, and so many other legendary players capable of dominating the field and inspiring millions around the world? In *Inspiring Stories of 21st Century Soccer Stars for Kids*, you'll find the answers to these questions and much more.

This book takes you inside the stories of some of the greatest players and national teams of the 21st century, revealing the secrets behind their success. Each of these stories demonstrates that behind every victory, record, or trophy, there's much more than just talent: there's dedication, perseverance, and the ability to overcome challenges.

From thrilling World Cup victories to historic moments in international leagues, these soccer champions have not only dominated the field but have also broken barriers and bridged cultures. Teams like Brazil, Spain, and the U.S. Women's National Team have shown that soccer is much more than just a game—it's a powerful force for diversity, inclusion, and unity. By sharing their journeys, this book highlights how soccer connects people from all walks of life and pushes them toward greatness.

You'll discover how these athletes have faced adversity and emerged as icons both on and off the field. Their stories reveal that success isn't simply about scoring goals or winning trophies; it's about mental toughness, embracing change, and finding new ways to improve—what we call the "secret formula" for becoming a soccer champion.

Beyond their on-field achievements, many of these athletes have used their fame to champion causes they care about, demonstrating that their influence goes far beyond the pitch. Whether through activism, philanthropy, or mentorship, these champions have proven that soccer can be a platform for making a positive impact in the world.

As you read through these pages, you'll also see how important values like ethics, fair play, and respect for opponents are in the lives of these champions. Their success is not just about winning—it's about playing with honor and integrity. They embody the true spirit of the game, and their stories are full of lessons that will inspire you to chase your own dreams.

Each story in this book explores the journey, struggles, and triumphs of soccer's biggest stars— from Messi's unmatched skill to Alex Morgan's clutch performances on the world's biggest stages. By unlocking the "secret formula" of these champions, you'll learn how passion, perseverance, and teamwork can help you reach new heights—not just in soccer, but in life.

Here are some of the legendary players you'll meet in this book:

- **Lionel Messi**: A eight-time Ballon d'Or winner, celebrated for his unmatched skill, vision, and consistency, making him one of the greatest players in soccer history.

- **Cristiano Ronaldo**: Known for his incredible goal-scoring ability, athleticism, and leadership, Ronaldo is a five-time Ballon d'Or winner who has left an indelible mark on both club and country.

- **Kaká**: The elegant Brazilian playmaker, a former Ballon d'Or winner, known for his vision and goal-scoring prowess, who has left his mark on both AC Milan and Real Madrid.

- **Carli Lloyd**: A two-time FIFA World Cup champion and two-time Olympic gold medalist, famous for her clutch performances and leadership in women's soccer.

- **Andrea Pirlo**: Revered for his football intelligence and passing, Pirlo was the architect behind Italy's success and a key player for Juventus and AC Milan.

- **Alex Morgan:** A two-time FIFA World Cup champion and Olympic gold medalist, Morgan is celebrated for her leadership on and off the field, pushing women's soccer to new heights.

- **Ronaldinho**: Known for his dazzling skills and infectious love for the game, the Brazilian magician brought joy and creativity to football, becoming a fan favorite globally.

- **Marta**: The Brazilian legend, often referred to as the greatest female player of all time, is a six-time FIFA World Player of the Year winner, known for her passion, resilience, and incredible skill, inspiring millions across the globe.

- **Zinedine Zidane**: Known for his incredible skill and composure, Zidane led France to World Cup glory in 1998 and found further success as a coach at Real Madrid.

- **Zlatan Ibrahimović**: An iconic striker with a commanding presence, technical skill, and a knack for scoring spectacular goals, Zlatan has become a global icon of modern football.

- **Megan Rapinoe**: A leader both on and off the pitch, Rapinoe has used her platform to advocate for social justice while excelling in international tournaments.

- **Luka Modrić**: The Croatian playmaker led his team to the 2018 World Cup final and won the Ballon d'Or for his vision, leadership, and exceptional passing ability.

- **Fabio Cannavaro**: A defensive genius, Cannavaro captained Italy to World Cup victory in 2006, winning the Ballon d'Or the same year for his outstanding performances.

- **Neymar**: Known for his flair, dribbling, and goal-scoring ability, Neymar continues to push the boundaries of soccer with his dazzling performances for Brazil and top European clubs.

Each of these players has not only excelled in their craft but has also embodied qualities that transcend the sport—resilience, leadership, and the power to inspire. Their inclusion in this book is a reflection of their extraordinary careers and the lasting impact they have had on the beautiful game. Whether through individual accolades like the Ballon d'Or, groundbreaking victories with national teams, or their ability to innovate and change the way the game is played, these athletes represent the pinnacle of soccer excellence in the 21st century.

As you delve into their stories, you'll discover not just the statistics and records that make these players stand out, but also the personal journeys, struggles, and triumphs that have shaped them into the legends they are today. Ready to unlock the secret formula? Let's begin!

LIONEL MESSI

The Magician of the Pitch

T he scene was set at the Santiago Bernabéu, the iconic home of Real Madrid, on a warm April evening in 2017. The atmosphere was electric, with over 80,000 fervent fans filling the stadium, their roars echoing through the air. This was El Clásico, the fiercest rivalry in football, pitting Barcelona against Real Madrid. It was more than just a game; it was a battle of pride, passion, and prestige. Barcelona needed a victory to keep their La Liga title hopes alive, but Real Madrid, led by Cristiano Ronaldo, were determined to assert their dominance. The tension was palpable as the players lined up, the weight of history pressing down on their shoulders.

As the match began, both teams displayed relentless intensity. Tackles flew in, and the game ebbed and flowed with breathtaking speed. The first half ended 1-1, with both sides trading blows like heavyweight boxers. Messi, as always, was at the heart of Barcelona's attack, weaving through defenders with his mesmerizing dribbles.

But it was in the second half that the legend of Lionel Messi truly ascended to mythical status. In the 77th minute, with the score locked at 2-2, Barcelona were reduced to ten men. The odds seemed stacked against them, but Messi's resolve only grew stronger.

In the 92nd minute, with the game nearing its end, Barcelona launched one final attack. Sergi Roberto embarked on a lung-bursting run from his own half, slicing through Real Madrid's midfield. The ball found its way to André Gomes, who calmly passed it to Jordi Alba. Alba, with the vision of a seasoned playmaker, spotted Messi's run and delivered a perfect pass to him on the edge of the box.

Time seemed to stand still as Messi, with the grace of a dancer, took one touch to control the ball and another to set himself. With a swish of his magical left foot, he curled the ball past Keylor Navas, sending it into the bottom corner of the net. The stadium fell silent for a moment, the realization of what had just happened sinking in.

Messi ran towards the corner flag, removing his shirt and holding it aloft to the stunned Madrid fans, his face a mask of triumph and defiance. It was a moment of pure, unadulterated emotion, a statement of his brilliance and determination. His teammates mobbed him, their jubilation palpable.

That night, Messi not only secured a crucial victory for Barcelona but also etched his name into the annals of football history. The image of him holding his shirt aloft became an iconic symbol of his legacy, a testament to his unparalleled genius and unyielding spirit. "This is why he's the best," Xavi Hernandez, watching from afar, remarked with admiration. "In moments of great pressure, Messi delivers magic."

Early Life and Discovery of Talent

In the bustling city of Rosario, Argentina, a young boy

named Lionel Messi was born on June 24, 1987, to Jorge and Celia Messi. From a very early age, it was clear that Lionel, or "Leo" as his family affectionately called him, was no ordinary child. He displayed an exceptional talent for football that set him apart from his peers. This talent was nurtured in a family that, despite their modest means, was deeply supportive of his passion.

Leo's father, Jorge Messi, worked in a steel factory while his mother, Celia, was employed part-time as a cleaner. Despite their modest means, the Messis were a close-knit family that nurtured Leo's passion for football. Jorge also coached a local youth team, and it was under his guidance that Leo first began to hone his skills. "You were born to play football, Leo," his father would often say, his voice filled with both pride and hope.

By the age of five, Messi was playing for a local club, Grandoli, where his grandmother Celia often accompanied him to training sessions and matches. Her unwavering belief in his talent was a constant source of encouragement. "One day, the whole world will know your name," she would say, her words carrying the conviction that only a loving grandmother could provide.

The Struggles Begin

Despite his prodigious talent, Messi faced significant challenges. At the age of 11, he was diagnosed with a growth hormone deficiency, a condition that required expensive treatment. His family's financial situation made it nearly impossible to afford the necessary medication. It was a dark period for the young boy, who feared that his dream of becoming a professional footballer might slip away.

However, fate intervened in the form of FC Barcelona. The club's scouts had heard of a young Argentine phenom and decided to give him a trial. Messi's performance at the trial was nothing short of spectacular, prompting Barcelona's technical director, Carles Rexach, to offer him a contract on a napkin, as no official documents were available at the moment. Barcelona also agreed to cover the cost of his medical treatment. This move to Spain marked the beginning of a new chapter in Messi's life.

Rising Through the Ranks

Joining Barcelona's famed La Masia academy, Messi found himself in a new environment, away from his family and friends. The transition was challenging, but the academy provided him with the best training and a new family in his teammates and coaches.

From the outset, Messi's talent was evident. He quickly moved up through the ranks, impressing everyone with his agility, vision, and uncanny ability to control the ball. Yet, it was not just his talent that set him apart but also his relentless work ethic. "Talent without hard work is nothing," Messi would often say, echoing the words of his father.

His La Masia coach, Víctor Valdés, once said, "Leo was always the first to arrive and the last to leave. His dedication was unmatched, and his passion for the game was evident in every training session."

Breakthrough and Early Success

Messi's breakthrough came on October 16, 2004, when

he made his debut for the senior team at just 17 years old. His initial appearances were marked by flashes of brilliance, and it was clear that a star was in the making. However, the path to stardom was not without its setbacks. Injuries plagued his early career, testing his resilience and determination.

Despite these obstacles, Messi's resolve never wavered. His dedication to recovery and improvement was unwavering. "Every setback is an opportunity to come back stronger," he would say, his eyes reflecting the steely determination that had become his trademark.

The Era of Dominance

By the 2008-2009 season, Messi had established himself as a key player for Barcelona. Under the guidance of coach Pep Guardiola, he flourished, helping the team to an unprecedented sextuple—winning six major trophies in a single year. Messi's performances were nothing short of spectacular, earning him the first of many Ballon d'Or awards.

Teammates and opponents alike marveled at his skills. Xavi Hernandez, a long-time teammate, once said, "Playing alongside Messi is like playing with the best player in the playground. You give him the ball, and you know something magical will happen."

The Words of Coaches and Teammates

Pep Guardiola, who coached Messi during some of his most prolific years, once remarked, "Messi is the best player I have ever seen. The difference between him and the others is his mindset. He is always looking to improve, never satisfied with what he has achieved."

Teammate Gerard Piqué shared a similar sentiment, "Training with Messi is an honor. He pushes everyone to be better. His humility and work ethic are what make him truly great."

A Remarkable Defeat and Redemption

While Messi's career has been filled with numerous triumphs, it has also seen significant defeats. One of the most memorable was the 2012 UEFA Champions League semi-final against Chelsea. Despite dominating possession and creating numerous chances, Barcelona were defeated. The loss was particularly painful as it happened in front of their home fans at Camp Nou. Messi himself missed a crucial penalty, hitting the crossbar. The defeat was a significant blow, and Messi was visibly distraught. "It was one of the hardest moments of my career," he admitted in an interview. "But such moments make you stronger."

The following season, Messi and Barcelona were determined to reclaim their glory. In the 2013-2014 season, they faced tough competition but showed remarkable resilience. Their determination culminated in an extraordinary victory in La Liga, where they clinched the title in dramatic fashion against Atletico Madrid. The season was a testament to their tenacity and Messi's leadership. "We learned from our defeat," Messi reflected. "It made us stronger and more united."

The Struggles of the National Team

While Messi's club career soared, success with the Argentine national team was more elusive. Despite his best efforts, the team fell short in several major tournaments, leading to criticism and doubt from the media and fans. The weight of expectations was immense, and the pressure took a toll on Messi.

In 2016, after yet another heartbreaking defeat in the Copa America final, Messi announced his retirement from international football. The decision was met with shock and disbelief. "I've tried so hard, but it seems I'm destined not to win with Argentina," he said, his voice heavy with disappointment.

The Comeback

The world of football rallied behind Messi, urging him to reconsider. Fans, players, and coaches alike recognized that his journey was far from over. After a period of reflection, Messi returned to the national team, driven by an unyielding desire to achieve success for his country.

His perseverance paid off in 2021 when Argentina won the Copa America, Messi's first major international trophy. The victory was a testament to his resilience and unwavering belief. "Never give up on your dreams, no matter how difficult the journey may be," Messi said, his voice filled with emotion.

Extraordinary Victories and Records

Messi's career has been marked by extraordinary victories and record-breaking performances. One of the most memorable moments came in the 2011-2012 season when he scored an astonishing 73 goals in all competitions, a feat that broke numerous records. His ability to perform at the highest level consistently earned him the admiration of fans and respect from peers worldwide.

Another highlight was the 2014-2015 season, where Messi, along with Neymar and Luis Suárez, formed the formidable attacking trio known as "MSN." Their chemistry on the field led Barcelona to a treble, winning La Liga, the Copa del Rey, and the UEFA Champions League. Andrés Iniesta, a key member of that team, said, "Leo's presence on the pitch lifts everyone's game. He makes us all believe that anything is possible."

Messi's Continued Pursuit of Excellence
Even as he enters the latter stages of his career, Messi's passion for football remains undiminished. His move to Paris Saint-Germain (PSG) in 2021 marked a new chapter, but his dedication to the sport and his desire to continue winning remained as strong as ever. PSG's head coach, Mauricio Pochettino, spoke highly of Messi's impact on the team, "Having Leo in the squad is a blessing. His presence lifts the entire team, and his commitment to excellence is infectious. He continues to set the standard for what it means to be a professional footballer."

Inter Miami: A New Chapter
In 2023, Messi made a surprising and significant move by joining Inter Miami, a Major League Soccer (MLS) team in the United States. His arrival in Miami was met with immense excitement and anticipation, not just from fans in the U.S., but from football enthusiasts worldwide.

Messi's debut with Inter Miami was nothing short of spectacular. On July 21, 2023, he played his first match against Cruz Azul in the Leagues Cup. With the score tied at 1-1 and the game entering stoppage time, Messi stepped up to take a free kick. With his characteristic precision and flair, he curled the ball into the top corner, securing a dramatic 2-1 victory for his new team. The crowd erupted, and Messi's legend continued to grow. "It felt like a fairytale," Messi said afterward. "To score in my debut and help the team win was a special moment."

Inter Miami's head coach, Phil Neville, praised Messi's immediate impact. "Having Leo in our team is transformative. His presence, his leadership, and his magic on the field are incredible. He's inspiring not just to the players, but to the entire community."

Messi's influence extended beyond the pitch. His presence in MLS brought unprecedented attention and viewership to the league. Young players across America began to dream bigger, inspired by the idea that the greatest player in the world was now playing in their backyard. "Watching Messi play in MLS makes me believe anything is possible," said a young fan from Miami. "He's a legend, and now he's here, showing us that our dreams can come true too."

Copa América 2024: A Crowning Glory

In 2024, Messi added another illustrious chapter to his career at the Copa América held in the United States. Despite struggling with a muscle injury, his leadership on and off the pitch was vital. Messi scored crucial goals and provided key assists, including one in the semifinal against Canada. His performance helped Argentina clinch the title, with Messi lifting the trophy in what was likely his final appearance in the tournament. This victory was a testament to his enduring skill and determination, further solidifying his legacy in the annals of football.

Final Reflections and Takeaway Message

Lionel Messi's career is a profound testament to perseverance, hard work, and the power of self-belief. From his early days in Rosario to becoming a global icon, Messi's journey has been a source of inspiration for millions. His story teaches young athletes that setbacks are an integral part of the journey, and true success lies in overcoming obstacles with determination.

Beyond his remarkable achievements on the pitch, Messi's humility and dedication extend to his efforts off the field. Through his foundation, he has provided countless opportunities for underprivileged children, driven by a deep desire to give back to the community that supported him. "I want to give back to the community that has given me so much," Messi has often said, underscoring his commitment to making a meaningful difference in the lives of others.

Reflecting on his journey, Messi frequently acknowledges the unwavering support of his family. "My family has been my rock," he says. "Without their support, I would not be where I am today. They have been with me through every high and low, and their belief in me has kept me going." This deep connection to his roots and the people who believed in him has been a cornerstone of his success.

Messi's story is a powerful reminder of what can be achieved when one dares to dream and works tirelessly to turn those dreams into reality. His journey from a young boy in Rosario to one of the greatest footballers of all time continues to inspire aspiring athletes worldwide. As Messi's legacy endures, it will undoubtedly inspire future generations to dream big and work relentlessly towards their goals.

In his own words, "You have to fight to reach your dream. You have to sacrifice and work hard for it." Messi's life and career exemplify the extraordinary outcomes that can be achieved through dedication, hard work, and the belief in oneself.

Key Takeaways from Messi's Story:

1. The Power of Determination

In 2017, during a crucial El Clásico match, Messi's determination led to a game-winning goal, solidifying his legendary status and demonstrating that resilience can lead to extraordinary achievements.

Takeaway: Never give up, even when the situation seems impossible.

2. Support from Loved Ones

Messi's talent was nurtured by his supportive family, especially his father and grandmother, despite financial difficulties.

Takeaway: Surround yourself with people who believe in you.

3. Overcoming Adversity

Diagnosed with a growth hormone deficiency at 11, Messi faced significant challenges but continued his dream with Barcelona's support.

Takeaway: Face challenges head-on and stay hopeful.

4. Hard Work and Dedication
Messi's relentless hard work and dedication led him to become one of the world's best, despite early struggles with injuries.
Takeaway: Talent is important, but hard work and dedication make the difference.

5. Learning from Defeat
After a painful loss to Chelsea in 2012, Messi used the experience to come back stronger, demonstrating the importance of learning from setbacks.
Takeaway: Every defeat is an opportunity to learn and grow.

6. National Team Perseverance
Despite challenges and criticism, Messi persisted with the Argentine national team and eventually led them to win the Copa America in 2021 and 2024.
Takeaway: Persistence pays off.

7. Continual Pursuit of Excellence
Even after achieving success, Messi sought new challenges with PSG and later Inter Miami, making an immediate impact.
Takeaway: Never stop striving for excellence.

8. Giving Back

Through his foundation, Messi provides opportunities for underprivileged children in education, healthcare, and sports.
Takeaway: Use your success to help others.

Final Motivational Message

Lionel Messi's journey from a young boy in Rosario to a football legend is a powerful reminder that with determination, hard work, and the support of loved ones, any dream is achievable. His story encourages us all to fight for our dreams, remain resilient in the face of adversity, and give back to others. No matter where you start, your journey can inspire countless others if you dare to dream big and work tirelessly to make those dreams a reality.

CRISTIANO RONALDO
The Relentless Conqueror

I t was a warm evening on June 24, 2014, when Real Madrid faced Atlético Madrid in the UEFA Champions League final. The Estádio da Luz in Lisbon was a cauldron of noise, with tens of thousands of fans on the edge of their seats. This was more than just a game; it was a clash for European supremacy, and Real Madrid was on the brink of securing their elusive 10th European title, known as "La Décima."

The tension was palpable as the players lined up. Every pass, every tackle, and every moment was amplified by the deafening roars of the crowd. Atlético Madrid, known for their tenacity and resilience, took an early lead through Diego Godín. As the clock ticked away, Real Madrid's hopes began to fade, and the atmosphere grew tense. Each second felt like an eternity for the Madridistas.

The minutes dragged on, and it seemed like Atlético would hold on to their slim lead. But Real Madrid's players, fueled by determination and the weight of their storied history, refused to surrender. The dying moments of the match were agonizing for fans and players alike. Then, in the 93rd minute, Sergio Ramos rose above everyone in the box to meet a corner kick with a powerful header. The ball soared past Atlético's goalkeeper, Thibaut Courtois, and nestled into the back of the net. The stadium erupted in a collective roar, a mixture of relief and euphoria. Ramos had done it. He had given Real Madrid a lifeline, sending the game into extra time.

The extra time period was a testament to Real Madrid's resilience and determination. With the score tied at 1-1, the match was poised on a knife-edge. The players were exhausted, their bodies pushed to the limit, but their spirits remained unbroken. It was Cristiano Ronaldo who stepped up to deliver the final blow. His lightning speed, remarkable strength, and pinpoint accuracy were on full display as he powered through Atlético's defense, creating opportunities and pushing his team forward.

In the 120th minute, as the match neared its conclusion, Ronaldo made one final surge into the box. He was brought down by Atlético's defenders, and the referee pointed to the spot. It was a penalty. With the weight of expectation on his shoulders, Ronaldo placed the ball on the spot. The entire stadium held its breath. Here was the moment that could define his legacy.

Ronaldo took a deep breath, his face a mask of concentration. He began his run-up and struck the ball with unerring precision. The ball flew into the net, past the outstretched hands of Courtois. The stadium erupted in an explosion of joy and relief. Ronaldo ripped off his shirt, flexing his muscles in a triumphant celebration. It was a moment of pure emotion, a testament to his brilliance and determination. Tears of joy streamed down his face as his teammates mobbed him.

Carlo Ancelotti, Real Madrid's coach at the time,

couldn't hold back his admiration. "This is why we call him the best," Ancelotti said, his voice filled with emotion. "He delivers when it matters most. His ability to rise to the occasion is unparalleled."

Teammate Iker Casillas, the legendary goalkeeper, echoed these sentiments. "Cristiano's goal was the culmination of our dream. He is a leader, a warrior, and a true champion. Moments like these are why he is considered one of the greatest."

For the fans, it was a night that would be etched in their memories forever. The celebrations went long into the night as Madridistas around the world rejoiced in their triumph. Ronaldo's heroics had secured "La Décima," and in doing so, he cemented his place in the pantheon of football legends.

Early Life and Discovery of Talent

Cristiano Ronaldo dos Santos Aveiro was born on February 5, 1985, on the island of Madeira, Portugal. Growing up in a modest neighborhood in Funchal, Ronaldo's early life was filled with challenges. His father, José Dinis Aveiro, worked as a municipal gardener and part-time kit man for a local football club, while his mother, Maria Dolores dos Santos Aveiro, was a cook. Despite their financial struggles, Ronaldo's family was close-knit and supportive.

From a young age, Ronaldo showed an extraordinary talent for football. He would often be seen playing in the streets with his friends, honing his skills and dreaming of a future in the sport. "Cristiano was always different," his mother would say. "He had a determination and drive that set him apart from other children."

By the age of eight, Ronaldo joined Andorinha, a local football club where his father worked. His talent was undeniable, and it wasn't long before he moved to Nacional, one of Madeira's top clubs. There, his skills continued to develop, and at the age of 12, he made the bold move to join Sporting Lisbon's youth academy, leaving his family behind to pursue his dreams.

The Struggles Begin

Moving to Lisbon was a daunting challenge for young Ronaldo, being far from family and facing tough competition. Despite the difficulties, his resolve remained strong. "I missed my family a lot," he said, "but I knew sacrifices were necessary for success." At Sporting Lisbon, his talent quickly stood out, making his first-team debut at 16 and impressing with his speed, skill, and scoring ability. His performances soon attracted the attention of Europe's top clubs.

The Big Move to Manchester United

In 2003, at the age of 18, Ronaldo made a high-profile move to Manchester United. The transfer fee of £12.24 million made him the most expensive teenager in English football history at the time. Under the guidance of Sir Alex Ferguson, Ronaldo's career reached new heights. Adapting to the physicality of the Premier League and the pressures of playing for such a prestigious club tested him. "It wasn't easy," he reflected. "But Sir Alex believed in me, and that gave me the confidence to push myself."

Rising to Stardom

By the 2006-2007 season, Ronaldo had established

himself as one of the Premier League's brightest stars. His dazzling footwork, blistering pace, and incredible goal-scoring ability made him a fan favorite. He played a pivotal role in helping Manchester United win three consecutive Premier League titles and the 2008 UEFA Champions League.

Teammate Wayne Rooney once said, "Playing with Cristiano was an honor. He was always pushing the limits, always striving to be the best. His work ethic was unmatched."

Sir Alex Ferguson, who played a crucial role in Ronaldo's development, often praised his work ethic and determination. "Cristiano was one of the most gifted players I've ever worked with," Ferguson said. "But it was his dedication and hunger to improve that made him truly special."

A Remarkable Defeat and Redemption

One of the most significant setbacks in Ronaldo's career came in the 2005-2006 season. Despite his brilliant performances, Manchester United were knocked out of the Champions League in the group stages, a humiliating exit for a club of their stature. Ronaldo was devastated, but this defeat fueled his determination to succeed.

The following season, Ronaldo came back stronger than ever. He led Manchester United to the Premier League title, scoring 17 goals and providing numerous assists. His redemption was complete when he scored in the Champions League final against Chelsea in 2008, helping United win their third European title. "The defeat taught me a lot," Ronaldo said. "It made me stronger and more determined to achieve my goals."

The Move to Real Madrid

In 2009, Ronaldo made a record-breaking transfer to Real Madrid for £80 million, making him the most expensive player in the world at the time. The pressure was immense, but Ronaldo thrived in the spotlight. His time at Real Madrid was marked by unprecedented success.

During his nine years at the club, Ronaldo won four Champions League titles, two La Liga titles, and numerous individual awards, including four Ballon d'Or trophies. His rivalry with Barcelona's Lionel Messi captivated football fans worldwide and pushed both players to new heights.

The Struggles of the National Team

While Ronaldo's club career soared, success with the Portuguese national team was more elusive. Despite his best efforts, Portugal often fell short in major tournaments, leading to criticism and doubt from the media and fans. The weight of expectations was immense, and the pressure took a toll on Ronaldo.

In the 2016 European Championship, Ronaldo faced yet another setback. He was forced to leave the final against France in tears due to injury. However, his leadership from the sidelines was inspirational, and Portugal went on to win their first major international trophy. "This victory is for all of Portugal," Ronaldo said, his voice filled with emotion. "We showed the world our strength and unity."

A New Challenge: Juventus

In 2018, Ronaldo made another bold move, joining Juventus in Italy's Serie A. The transfer shocked the football world, but Ronaldo was determined to prove himself in a new league. His impact was immediate, helping Juventus win two consecutive Serie A titles and continuing to break records.

The Return to Manchester United: A Homecoming
In 2021, Ronaldo made a sensational return to Manchester United. The news was met with immense excitement from fans and players alike. "It's like coming home," Ronaldo said. "I have so many great memories here, and I'm excited to create new ones."
Ronaldo's second stint at Manchester United started with a bang. On September 11, 2021, he scored two goals on his return to Old Trafford, helping his team to a 4-1 victory over Newcastle United. His presence invigorated the squad and brought renewed hope to the fans. "Cristiano's return has been like a dream," said Ole Gunnar Solskjær, the manager at the time. "He has an incredible ability to inspire those around him."

Al Nassr: A New Adventure in Saudi Arabia
In December 2022, Cristiano Ronaldo began a new chapter by joining Al Nassr in the Saudi Pro League. This bold move into a less prominent league offered an opportunity to expand his global influence. At his unveiling, Ronaldo stated, "Football has no boundaries, and neither do I," expressing his desire to help grow the sport in Saudi Arabia. His impact was immediate, both on and off the pitch, attracting attention to the league and inspiring local players. Al

Nassr coach Rudi Garcia praised Ronaldo for bringing professionalism and leadership, quickly becoming a fan favorite with his crucial performances.

Final Reflections and Takeaway Messages

Reflecting on his journey, Cristiano Ronaldo highlights perseverance and the unwavering support of his family. "My family has been my rock," he says, crediting them for his success. Ronaldo's story is one of hard work, dedication, and self-belief, inspiring athletes worldwide. From his beginnings in Madeira to becoming one of football's greatest, his legacy encourages future generations to dream big and work relentlessly. As Ronaldo himself puts it, "Your love makes me strong, your hate makes me unstoppable," a testament to the power of resilience and determination.

Cristiano Ronaldo's journey offers several key lessons and inspirational messages:

1. Perseverance and Resilience

Despite immense pressure and the possibility of defeat in the Champions League final, Ronaldo and his team refused to give up, ultimately securing a historic victory.

Takeaway: Never give up, no matter how tough the circumstances. Face challenges head-on and believe in your ability to overcome them.

2. Dedication and Hard Work

From his early days playing in the streets of Madeira to becoming a global football star, Ronaldo's success is rooted in relentless dedication and hard work.

Takeaway: Success is built on a foundation of hard work and relentless practice. Dedicate time and effort to your passions.

3. Overcoming Setbacks
After a significant defeat in the Champions League, Ronaldo used the experience to fuel his determination, leading his team to victory the following season.
Takeaway: Setbacks are opportunities to come back stronger. View failures as learning experiences and use them to build resilience.

4. Embracing New Challenges
Ronaldo's move to different leagues and teams showcased his adaptability and desire to continuously improve.
Takeaway: Embrace new opportunities and challenges. They can lead to personal growth and unexpected successes.

Final Motivational Message
Cristiano Ronaldo's rise from a modest neighborhood in Madeira to one of football's greatest is a testament to hard work, perseverance, and self-belief. His journey inspires others to chase their dreams, overcome challenges, and pursue excellence. Ronaldo's story shows that success isn't just about talent—it's about the determination to make dreams a reality.

KAKA'

The Prince of Football

The 2014 FIFA World Cup final was held in the iconic Maracanã Stadium in Rio de Janeiro. It was a match that would go down in history, and for Kakà, it was the moment that would cement his legacy as one of football's greatest legends.

Brazil faced Germany, and the atmosphere was electric. The stadium was a sea of yellow and green, with fans cheering and waving flags, united in their hope for a Brazilian victory. Kakà, at the age of 32, was the captain of the Brazilian national team. Though many considered him to be past his prime, Kakà's experience and leadership were invaluable to the squad. He had announced that this would be his last World Cup, and he was determined to lead his team to glory.

The match began with both teams playing cautiously, aware of the high stakes. Germany's midfield was formidable, but Kakà, with his trademark elegance and vision, orchestrated Brazil's attacks. In the 27th minute, Kakà received the ball just outside the penalty area. With a deft touch, he dribbled past two German defenders and unleashed a powerful shot that curled into the top corner of the net. The Maracanã erupted in jubilation as Brazil took the lead. "Scoring that goal felt like a dream," Kakà later recalled. "The roar of the crowd, the joy on my teammates' faces—it was unforgettable."

Germany responded with relentless pressure, and in the 65th minute, they equalized with a well-placed header. The match was now tied, and the tension in the stadium was palpable. Kakà, despite feeling the physical toll of the game, continued to inspire his team. His precise passes and strategic positioning kept Brazil in the fight.

As the match approached its final minutes, extra time seemed inevitable. But in the 88th minute, Kakà made a decisive move. He intercepted a pass in the midfield and launched a swift counterattack. Sprinting towards the German goal, he played a one-two with Neymar, receiving the ball back inside the box. With the German defense scrambling, Kakà chipped the ball over the advancing goalkeeper, securing a dramatic late goal. The Maracanã exploded with joy, and Kakà was mobbed by his ecstatic teammates. "In that moment, I felt like I was flying," Kakà said. "It was pure ecstasy, knowing we were so close to victory."

Germany desperately tried to equalize in the dying minutes, but Brazil's defense held firm. The final whistle blew, and Brazil were crowned World Cup champions. Kakà, overwhelmed with emotion, fell to his knees and thanked God for the victory. It was a match that would go down in history, and for Kakà, who led his team to the pinnacle of football, it was the moment that would cement his legacy as one of football's greatest legends.

Early Life and the Spark of Passion

In the bustling city of Brasília, Brazil, a young boy named Ricardo Izecson dos Santos Leite—known to the world as Kakà—began a journey that would take him from the streets of his hometown to the grandest stages of international football.

Kakà was born on April 22, 1982, into a supportive and loving family. His father, Bosco Izecson Pereira Leite, was an engineer, and his mother, Simone dos Santos, was an elementary school teacher. Growing up in a middle-class family, Kakà had the privilege of a stable and nurturing environment. From an early age, he displayed a keen interest in sports, particularly football, which is a passion shared by many Brazilian youngsters.

"I remember my first football," Kakà once recalled in an interview. "It was a small, worn-out ball, but to me, it was the world. I would spend hours kicking it around in our backyard, dreaming of playing in big stadiums." At seven years old, Kakà joined his local club, Alphaville. His natural talent was evident even then. He possessed a rare combination of speed, agility, and vision, making him stand out among his peers. His coaches and teammates often marveled at his ability to read the game and execute precise passes. His first coach, Rubén Gonzalez, once said, "Kakà had an innate understanding of the game. Even at such a young age, he had the vision and the skills of a seasoned player."

Overcoming Early Setbacks

Despite his promising talent, Kakà's journey was not without its challenges. At the age of 18, he suffered a severe spinal fracture in a swimming pool accident.

The injury was potentially career-ending, and for a time, it seemed like his dreams of becoming a professional footballer might be shattered.

"I was scared," Kakà admitted. "There were moments when I thought I might never play football again. But my faith and the support of my family kept me going." Kakà turned to his faith, praying for strength and recovery. His parents were his pillars of support, ensuring he received the best medical care and rehabilitation. Slowly but surely, Kakà regained his strength and returned to the pitch. This period of adversity shaped his character, instilling in him a resilience that would define his career.

"I learned that setbacks are just setups for comebacks," Kakà often shared. "Every injury, every defeat taught me something valuable. It made me stronger, both physically and mentally."

Rising Star at São Paulo FC

Kakà's perseverance paid off when he signed with São Paulo FC, one of Brazil's most prestigious football clubs. He quickly rose through the ranks, making his professional debut in 2001. His performances were nothing short of spectacular. In his first full season, Kakà scored 12 goals in 27 matches, helping São Paulo win the Torneio Rio-São Paulo championship.

"Kakà was a joy to coach," said Oswaldo de Oliveira, his coach at São Paulo. "He was always eager to learn, always willing to put in the extra effort. His dedication was remarkable, and it was clear from the beginning that he was destined for greatness."

His stellar performances caught the attention of European scouts. In 2003, Kakà made a life-changing move to AC Milan for a transfer fee of €8.5 million. Despite the pressure of playing for one of the biggest clubs in the world, Kakà thrived.

Triumphs and Challenges at AC Milan

At AC Milan, Kakà's career reached new heights. His vision, creativity, and goal-scoring ability made him an integral part of the team. In 2004, he helped Milan win the Serie A title. The pinnacle of his success came in 2007 when he led Milan to victory in the UEFA Champions League, scoring crucial goals and providing key assists throughout the tournament.

Reflecting on that season, Kakà said, "It was a dream come true. Winning the Champions League with Milan was one of the greatest moments of my life. The hard work, the sacrifices—it all paid off."

His coach at Milan, Carlo Ancelotti, had immense respect for Kakà. "Kakà is one of those players who make coaching a pleasure. His professionalism, his dedication, and his humility are exemplary. He has the heart of a champion and the spirit of a leader," Ancelotti often remarked.

Kakà's teammate at Milan, Paolo Maldini, noted, "Kakà's resilience is what sets him apart. No matter how tough things got, he always came back with a smile and a renewed determination to succeed. His positive attitude was contagious and inspired all of us."

However, Kakà's journey was not devoid of hardships. The physical demands of top-level football took a toll on his body. Injuries became a frequent companion, challenging his ability to perform consistently. Yet, each setback only fueled his determination to return stronger.

One of Kakà's rivals, Francesco Totti of AS Roma, once said, "Playing against Kakà was always a challenge. He had this incredible ability to change the game in an instant. Even when he was not at his best physically, his mind was always sharp, and his heart was always in the game."

A Hero's Welcome at Real Madrid

In 2009, Kakà made another significant move, this time to Real Madrid, for a then-world record transfer fee of €67 million. His time at Madrid was marked by both triumphs and tribulations. He won the Copa del Rey in 2011 and La Liga in 2012, but persistent injuries hampered his ability to showcase his true potential.

Despite the challenges, Kakà remained a beloved figure among fans and teammates. His humility, work ethic, and positive attitude endeared him to many. "Kakà is not just a great player; he's a great person," said Cristiano Ronaldo, one of his teammates at Madrid. "He always puts the team first and inspires us with his dedication."

Kakà's coach at Real Madrid, José Mourinho, also had high praise for him. "Kakà is the epitome of professionalism. He faced many difficulties with injuries, but he never lost his spirit or his commitment to the team. He is a true role model for young players," Mourinho stated.

A Remarkable Defeat and Glorious Redemption

One of the most notable moments in Kakà's career was the 2005 UEFA Champions League final, where AC Milan faced Liverpool. Milan went into halftime with a commanding 3-0 lead, with Kakà providing a brilliant assist. However, in one of the most dramatic comebacks in football history, Liverpool scored three goals in the second half and eventually won the match on penalties.

"It was heartbreaking," Kakà recalled. "We were so close to winning, and to lose like that was devastating. It took a lot to recover from that defeat."

The pain of that loss lingered, but Kakà and his Milan teammates used it as motivation. Two years later, in the 2007 UEFA Champions League final, Milan faced Liverpool once again. This time, Kakà played a pivotal role, providing an assist and orchestrating the midfield with his trademark elegance and vision. Milan emerged victorious with a 2-1 win, securing their redemption.

"Winning the Champions League in 2007 was a moment of pure joy and relief," Kakà said. "We had carried the weight of that 2005 defeat with us, and to come back and win against the same team was incredibly satisfying."

Carlo Ancelotti praised Kakà's contribution: "Kakà was instrumental in our victory. His performance was a testament to his resilience and his ability to rise to the occasion."

Returning Home and Legacy

In 2013, Kakà returned to AC Milan, hoping to rekindle his magic at the club where he had enjoyed so much success. Although his second stint was not as illustrious as the first, Kakà continued to display flashes of brilliance and leadership.

One memorable match was against Lazio in 2014, where Kakà scored twice in a 3-0 victory, showcasing that his talent and passion for the game were still very much alive. "That game was special," Kakà reflected. "It felt like I was back in my prime, doing what I love most."

After his time at Milan, Kakà concluded his professional career with Orlando City SC in Major League Soccer (MLS), where he played from 2014 to 2017. His presence in MLS brought increased attention to the league, and he continued to inspire young players with his skill and sportsmanship.

"Kakà brought a level of class and professionalism to our club that was truly inspiring," said Adrian Heath, Kakà's coach at Orlando City SC. "He was a leader on and off the pitch, always willing to mentor younger players and share his knowledge."

Inspirational Moments and Quotes

Throughout his career, Kakà was known for his inspirational quotes and interviews. One of his most famous sayings is, "I play for God. My aim is to play football to bring joy to people, and for that, I thank God every day."

In an interview with ESPN, Kakà reflected on his journey: "Football has given me so much, but it's not just about the trophies or the fame. It's about the journey, the people I've met, the lessons I've learned. I hope my story can inspire others to pursue their dreams, no matter how difficult the path may be."

Kakà's mother, Simone, often shared her pride in her son's achievements. "Ricardo has always been a dedicated and humble boy. His faith and perseverance have guided him through the toughest times. We are incredibly proud of him," she said in an interview.

His father, Bosco, added, "From a young age, Ricardo

showed a deep love for football. We supported him, but it was his determination and faith that carried him through the challenges. Watching him achieve his dreams has been one of the greatest joys of our lives."

Final Reflection and Takeaway Message
Kakà's story is a testament to faith, hard work, and perseverance. From Brasília to European football's grand stages, he overcame significant challenges, including a career-threatening injury, with determination and self-belief. Beyond his on-field success, Kakà's leadership, humility, and commitment to giving back have made a lasting impact on football and society. His journey emphasizes the importance of embracing passion, staying humble, and turning adversity into opportunity. Kakà's example of leadership and dedication shows how success can positively impact others, with his unwavering faith guiding him to the top.

Key Takeaways from Kakà's Story:

1. Embrace Your Passion and Excel
From a young age, Kakà's love for football drove him to spend countless hours practicing and dreaming of greatness. His dedication to his passion led him to achieve remarkable success on the global stage. *Takeaway: Find what you love and commit to it wholeheartedly. Passion fuels excellence.*

2. Overcome Adversity with Determination
At 18, Kakà faced a severe spinal injury that threatened his football career. Relying on his faith

and family support, he overcame this challenge and returned stronger.

Takeaway: When faced with obstacles, use determination and resilience to turn setbacks into comebacks.

3. Work Hard and Stay Humble

Throughout his career at São Paulo, AC Milan, and Real Madrid, Kakà's work ethic and humility were evident. He consistently sought to learn and improve. Takeaway: Hard work and humility are keys to continuous growth and success.

4. Transform Defeats into Motivation

The painful loss in the 2005 UEFA Champions League final motivated Kakà and his team to return and triumph in 2007.

Takeaway: Use your defeats as motivation to strive for even greater victories.

5. Lead by Example

Kakà's leadership on and off the field inspired his teammates and coaches. His professionalism and dedication set a high standard.

Takeaway: Lead through actions and inspire others with your commitment and integrity.

6. Stay Positive and Resilient

Despite facing numerous injuries, Kakà's positive attitude and resilience allowed him to overcome challenges and perform at the highest level.

Takeaway: Maintain a positive mindset and resilience to navigate and overcome difficulties.

7. Trust in Yourself and Your Faith
Kakà's unwavering faith played a crucial role in his journey, guiding him through tough times and fueling his success.
Takeaway: Believe in yourself and your journey, and let faith guide you through challenges.

Final Motivational Message
Kakà's story exemplifies the power of passion, perseverance, and humility. His journey from a young boy in Brasília to a global football icon shows that with hard work, faith, and resilience, anything is possible.

As you pursue your dreams, remember these lessons from Kakà's life. Embrace your passions, overcome adversity, work hard, stay humble, use defeats as motivation, lead by example, stay positive, give back to your community, and trust in yourself and your faith.

"Never give up on your dreams. Work hard, stay humble, and trust in yourself. There will be challenges, but with faith and perseverance, you can overcome anything." – Kakà

CARLI LLOYD
The Heart of a Champion

In the quiet suburb of Delran Township, New Jersey, a young girl named Carli Lloyd began her journey towards becoming one of the most revered soccer players in the world. Born on July 16, 1982, Carli's early life was marked by her exceptional talent and a relentless work ethic that would later define her illustrious career. From her childhood days, kicking a soccer ball around with her siblings, to standing on the grand stages of the World Cup and the Olympics, Carli Lloyd's story is one of perseverance, dedication, and an unyielding belief in her dreams.

Early Life and the Seeds of Passion

Carli's parents, Stephen and Pamela Lloyd, noticed her natural affinity for soccer at a young age. By the time she was five, Carli was already displaying a remarkable ability to control and distribute the ball. Her mother, Pamela, often reminisced about those early days, saying, "At that age, it was coed, and Carli was hanging with the boys. She always loved it and showed a lot of ability from an early age, but she also has always worked hard".

Carli's high school years at Delran High School were transformative. Under the mentorship of the late Rudy

"The Red Baron" Klobach, she honed her skills and emerged as a standout player. Her senior year was particularly impressive, as she captained her team to an 18-3 record, scoring 26 goals and providing eight assists. She was twice named the Philadelphia Inquirer's Girls' High School Player of the Year and earned Parade All-American honors in 1999 and 2000. Coach Rudy Klobach was a significant influence in Carli's early development. He saw potential in her that extended beyond her physical abilities. "Carli had a vision on the field that you don't see often at that age," Klobach once said. "She was always thinking two steps ahead, planning her next move before anyone else on the pitch even realized what was happening."

Collegiate Success and Early Challenges

Continuing her soccer journey, Carli attended Rutgers University, where she played for the Scarlet Knights women's soccer team from 2001 to 2004. Her collegiate career was marked by significant achievements, including being named First-Team All-Big East for four consecutive years. Despite her growing success, Carli faced numerous challenges. Balancing academics and athletics was no easy feat, but she managed to excel in both, ending her college career with 117 points and 50 goals.

During her time at Rutgers, Carli's coach, Glenn Crooks, played a pivotal role in shaping her as a player. "Carli was always the first to arrive and the last to leave," Crooks recalled. "Her dedication was unparalleled. She was constantly looking for ways to improve, whether it was through extra training sessions or studying the tactics of the game."

Breaking Through to the National Team

Carli's transition to professional soccer was not without its hurdles. She played for various teams in the Women's Professional Soccer (WPS) league, including the Chicago Red Stars, Sky Blue FC, and the Atlanta Beat, before finding her footing. Her big break came when she was selected for the U.S. Women's National Team (USWNT) in 2005. However, her initial years with the national team were a test of her resilience and determination.

Olympic Glory and World Cup Triumphs

Carli's defining moments came during the Olympics and World Cup tournaments. At the 2008 Beijing Olympics, she scored the game-winning goal in the final against Brazil, securing the gold medal for the U.S. team. Reflecting on that moment, Carli said, "It's all about the struggle because without it, there would be no truly great moments". She repeated her heroics at the 2012 London Olympics, scoring both goals in a 2-1 victory over Japan in the final.

Her crowning achievement came in the 2015 FIFA Women's World Cup. Carli delivered a performance for the ages, scoring a hat trick in the final against Japan, with her third goal coming from midfield. This extraordinary feat earned her the Golden Ball as the tournament's best player and solidified her legacy as one of the greatest soccer players of all time.

Her teammates and rivals alike have often spoken of her incredible drive. "Carli is a force of nature," said fellow USWNT star Alex Morgan. "Her work ethic is second to none, and she always steps up when it matters the most." Japanese player Aya Miyama, who faced Lloyd in several key matches, once noted, "Playing against Carli is always a challenge. She's relentless and has a knack for turning games on their head."

Overcoming Adversity and Seeking Redemption
One of Carli Lloyd's most significant moments of adversity came in the 2011 FIFA Women's World Cup. The U.S. team, despite a strong start, faced a heartbreaking defeat against Japan in the final. The match ended in a 2-2 draw after extra time, leading to a penalty shootout that Japan won 3-1. It was a crushing blow for the team, and for Carli personally.
Determined to redeem herself and her team, Carli used this defeat as fuel for her future successes. Just a year later, at the 2012 London Olympics, the U.S. faced Japan once again in the final. This time, Carli Lloyd delivered a masterful performance, scoring both goals in a 2-1 victory. "That loss in 2011 was tough, but it made us stronger. We came back more determined, and winning gold in 2012 felt like the perfect redemption," Carli said.

Resilience, Advocacy, and Legacy
Carli Lloyd's career is a powerful testament to resilience, hard work, and unwavering belief in oneself. Despite facing criticism, injuries, and self-doubt, she never wavered in her pursuit of excellence, embodying her mantra, "Never give up. Never quit." Beyond her on-field triumphs, Carli has been a vocal advocate for gender equality, using her platform to fight for equal pay and inspire countless young athletes. Her legacy,

marked by her dedication to improvement and advocacy for fairness, continues to inspire even in her retirement.

Final Reflections and Takeaway Message
In her own words, Carli encapsulates the essence of her journey: "If you have a dream, then your dream is attainable through hard work, sacrifice, and dedication. It might not be easy, and it might not happen right away, but this is what it takes to make your dream a reality".
Carli Lloyd's story is a beacon of hope and inspiration for young athletes around the world. It reminds us all that with perseverance, dedication, and a relentless pursuit of our dreams, anything is possible.

Key Takeaways from Carli's Story:

1. The Power of Determination
In 2015, during the FIFA Women's World Cup final, Carli's determination led to a historic hat trick, solidifying her legendary status and demonstrating that resilience can lead to extraordinary achievements.
Takeaway: Never give up, even when the situation seems impossible.

2. Support from Loved Ones
Carli's talent was nurtured by her supportive family, especially her parents, despite various challenges.
Takeaway: Surround yourself with people who believe in you.

3. Overcoming Adversity
Facing criticism and self-doubt, Carli continued her dream with unwavering determination and the support of her coaches.
Takeaway: Face challenges head-on and stay hopeful.

4. Hard Work and Dedication
Carli's relentless hard work and dedication led her to become one of the world's best, despite early struggles and injuries.
Takeaway: Talent is important, but hard work and dedication make the difference.

5. Learning from Defeat
After a painful loss in the 2011 Women's World Cup final, Carli used the experience to come back stronger, demonstrating the importance of learning from setbacks.
Takeaway: Every defeat is an opportunity to learn and grow.

6. Giving Back
Through her clinics and motivational speaking, Carli provides opportunities for young athletes to learn and grow.
Takeaway: Use your success to help others.

7. Inspiration to Others
Carli's story inspires countless young athletes with her humility, dedication, and relentless pursuit of dreams.
Takeaway: Let your journey inspire others.

8. Family Support and Humility

Carli credits her family's support and emphasizes humility and dedication in achieving her dreams.

Takeaway: Stay humble and appreciate those who support you.

Final Motivational Message

Carli Lloyd's journey from a young girl in Delran to a soccer legend is a testament to the power of determination, hard work, and the support of loved ones. Her story shows that success isn't just about talent but the relentless pursuit of excellence. Despite numerous obstacles, Carli used challenges as motivation, demonstrating that with perseverance and self-belief, anything is possible. For young athletes and dreamers, her career is a beacon of hope, reminding us that dreams are within reach if you work tirelessly and stay committed. As Carli says, "You have to fight to reach your dream. You have to sacrifice and work hard for it." Her legacy will continue to inspire future generations to pursue their passions and achieve greatness.

ANDREA PIRLO
The Maestro's Journey

In the small town of Flero, Brescia, Italy, a young boy named Andrea Pirlo discovered his passion for football. Born on May 19, 1979, to a family that appreciated sports, Andrea found solace and joy in the simple act of kicking a ball. Little did anyone know that this quiet, introspective child would one day become one of the most revered footballers of all time, known as "Il Maestro" for his unparalleled vision, technique, and grace on the field.

The Birth of a Passion

As a child, Andrea Pirlo spent countless hours playing football in the streets with his older brother, Ivan. The Pirlo family lived modestly, and their father, Luigi, ran a metal trading company. Despite the family's limited resources, Andrea's parents supported their sons' love for football, understanding the joy and discipline it brought into their lives.

"Andrea was always different," Ivan would later recall in an interview. "He had this incredible focus and calmness, even as a child. When he played, it was like he was in another world."

At the age of nine, Andrea joined the local club Flero, where his talents quickly became apparent. His ability to read the game and his exceptional ball control set him apart from his peers. Coaches and spectators alike marveled at his natural ability, predicting great things for the young midfielder.

Challenges and Triumphs: The Path to Professionalism

Despite his evident talent, Andrea's journey to professional football was not without its challenges. He faced stiff competition and the ever-present possibility of injury. At the age of 13, he moved to Brescia's youth academy, a significant step up in his budding career. Here, the competition was fiercer, and the pressure to perform was immense.

Andrea's dedication never wavered. He trained relentlessly, honing his skills and developing his unique playing style. "Football is not just a game for me," Andrea once said. "It's a way of life. Every pass, every touch, it all matters."

His hard work paid off when, at the age of 16, he made his debut for Brescia's senior team. It was a moment of immense pride and also a testament to his perseverance. However, his early professional years were marked by inconsistency and self-doubt. Despite his obvious talent, Andrea struggled to find his place in a team full of seasoned professionals.

The Move to Inter Milan and Rebirth at AC Milan

In 1998, Andrea Pirlo's career took a significant turn when he signed with Inter Milan. However, his time at Inter was challenging. He found it difficult to secure a regular spot in the first team and was often loaned out to other clubs. These years were frustrating for

Andrea, who knew he had the potential to be a key player but struggled to prove himself.

In 2001, Andrea moved to AC Milan, a transfer that would redefine his career. Under the guidance of manager Carlo Ancelotti, Pirlo was transformed from an attacking midfielder to a deep-lying playmaker. This change allowed him to fully utilize his vision, passing accuracy, and game intelligence. It was a masterstroke that unlocked Pirlo's potential and set him on the path to greatness.

"Andrea sees football differently from everyone else," Ancelotti once remarked. "He can read the game like a book and knows exactly where to place the ball to change the course of a match."

Pirlo flourished at Milan, becoming the heartbeat of the team. His performances helped the club win two Serie A titles, two UEFA Champions League titles, and a host of other trophies. His ability to control the tempo of the game and deliver precise, game-changing passes earned him the nickname "Il Maestro."

One of the most memorable moments of Pirlo's career came during the 2005 UEFA Champions League final against Liverpool, known as the "Miracle of Istanbul." Despite Milan's devastating loss after leading 3-0 at halftime, Pirlo's resilience and performance were praised. "It was one of the hardest moments in my career," Pirlo said. "But it taught me the importance of never giving up, no matter how dire the situation seems."

Remarkable Defeat and Sweet Revenge:
The 2005 UEFA Champions League final in Istanbul remains one of the most remarkable and

heartbreaking defeats in football history. AC Milan led Liverpool 3-0 at halftime, with Pirlo playing a crucial role in orchestrating Milan's dominance. However, in a stunning turnaround, Liverpool scored three goals in the second half and eventually won the match on penalties.

Pirlo later described the defeat as a dark moment in his career. "After Istanbul, I seriously thought about quitting football," he admitted. "It was a nightmare. We were so close to glory, and it slipped away. But the pain of that defeat fueled a fire within me to come back stronger."

Two years later, in 2007, Milan had the chance to exact revenge. They faced Liverpool once again in the Champions League final, this time in Athens. Pirlo was determined to rewrite the narrative. With a commanding performance, he controlled the midfield and provided the assist for Filippo Inzaghi's opening goal. Milan won the match 2-1, and Pirlo lifted the trophy that had eluded them in Istanbul.

"This victory was about redemption," Pirlo said. "It was about proving to ourselves that we could overcome adversity. The taste of victory was sweeter because of the pain we endured."

International Glory and Personal Struggles

Andrea's success at the club level was mirrored by his achievements with the Italian national team. He played a pivotal role in Italy's triumph at the 2006 FIFA World Cup, providing crucial assists and demonstrating his calmness under pressure. His performance in the final against France, where he coolly converted a penalty in the shootout, was a testament to his mental fortitude.

Fabio Cannavaro, Italy's captain during the World Cup, often spoke highly of Pirlo's influence. "Andrea was the brain of our team. His vision and precision were unmatched. We knew that with him on the pitch, anything was possible."

However, Pirlo's career was not without its setbacks. Injuries and personal struggles tested his resilience. In 2011, after a decade with AC Milan, he made the surprising decision to join Juventus. Many doubted his ability to adapt and thrive in a new environment at the age of 32. Yet, Andrea proved his critics wrong, leading Juventus to four consecutive Serie A titles and solidifying his legacy as one of the greatest midfielders of all time.

"Age is just a number," Andrea would often say. "What matters is how you feel and how much you are willing to give to the game."

The Final Chapter: Transition to Coaching

As his playing days ended, Andrea Pirlo knew he wanted to stay connected to the game. In 2017, he retired, leaving a legacy of brilliance and inspiration, but his football journey was far from over. In 2020, he became the head coach of Juventus, transitioning from player to coach, driven by a desire to share his deep understanding of the game with the next generation. "Coaching is a different kind of challenge," Andrea said. "But it's an opportunity to shape young players and help them achieve their dreams." As a coach, he emphasized intelligence, creativity, and composure, earning respect for his calm presence and ability to connect with players.

Extraordinary Victories and Moments of Brilliance

Andrea Pirlo's career is dotted with extraordinary victories and moments of brilliance that highlight his exceptional talent and unyielding determination. One such moment was the 2003 UEFA Champions League final against Juventus, where Pirlo's precise passing and composure under pressure were instrumental in Milan's victory. His assist for Andriy Shevchenko's decisive penalty in the shootout showcased his ability to perform in the most intense situations.

Another defining moment came during the 2012 European Championship, where Pirlo's masterful performances guided Italy to the final. His unforgettable Panenka penalty against England in the quarter-finals epitomized his calmness and audacity. England goalkeeper Joe Hart later admitted, "Pirlo's penalty was pure class. It takes a lot of courage to do that in such a crucial moment."

Teammates and rivals alike have spoken of Pirlo's genius on the field. Gianluigi Buffon, his long-time friend and teammate, once said, "Andrea is a genius. Playing with him is a privilege because he can see and execute passes that others can't even imagine."

Impact Beyond the Pitch

Andrea Pirlo's influence extends beyond his on-field achievements. He has become a role model for young players around the world, demonstrating that intelligence, creativity, and hard work are just as important as physical prowess. His autobiography, "I Think Therefore I Play," offers insights into his philosophy and approach to the game, inspiring countless readers.

Pirlo's commitment to giving back to the community is also noteworthy. Through various charitable initiatives, he has worked to provide opportunities for underprivileged children to access sports and education. His efforts have made a significant impact, showing that true greatness is measured not only by personal success but also by the positive change one brings to others.

Final Reflections and Takeaway Message

Andrea Pirlo's rise from a young boy in Flero to a footballing legend is a testament to passion, perseverance, and belief. His career, marked by triumphs and challenges, illustrates that success requires more than talent—it demands hard work, resilience, and the courage to overcome obstacles. Pirlo's journey teaches young athletes that true greatness lies in rising above adversity and striving for excellence. As his former coach Carlo Ancelotti said, "Andrea Pirlo is a true maestro, not just in football but in life," embodying the power of passion and perseverance.

Key Takeaways from Andrea Pirlo's Story:

1. Find Your Passion and Dedicate Yourself Fully
From a young age, Andrea Pirlo displayed an immense love for football. His dedication to the sport was evident in his relentless practice and desire to improve.
Takeaway: Find what you love and commit to it

wholeheartedly. Passion is the driving force behind success.

2. Persevere Through Adversity

Pirlo's journey was not without challenges. From struggling to secure a spot in Inter Milan's first team to facing a heartbreaking defeat in the 2005 UEFA Champions League final, Andrea experienced significant setbacks. He used these experiences to fuel his determination and come back stronger.
Takeaway: Adversity is a part of life. Persevere and use setbacks as motivation to achieve greater success.

3. Develop Resilience and Mental Fortitude

The ability to stay calm and composed under pressure is a hallmark of Pirlo's career. His performance in crucial moments, such as the 2006 World Cup final and the 2012 European Championship, showcases his mental strength.
Takeaway: Develop resilience and mental fortitude to handle stress and perform at your best when it matters most.

4. Embrace Continuous Improvement

Despite his natural talent, Pirlo never stopped learning and refining his skills. His transformation under Carlo Ancelotti at AC Milan into a deep-lying playmaker exemplifies his willingness to adapt and improve.
Takeaway: Always strive for continuous improvement and be open to learning new things. Adaptability is key to long-term success.

5. Lead and Inspire Others

Pirlo's calm demeanor and wisdom made him a natural leader and mentor. He inspired and guided younger players, sharing his experiences and knowledge.

Takeaway: Leadership is about lifting others up and being a positive influence. Strive to be a role model in every aspect of your life.

Final Motivational Message

Andrea Pirlo's story is a shining example of what can be achieved with passion, perseverance, and an unwavering belief in oneself. No matter where you come from or the challenges you face, you have the power to shape your destiny.

As Andrea Pirlo himself once said, "You have to believe in your dreams and work hard to make them come true. There will be obstacles, but they are there to be overcome." Let this message inspire you to pursue your dreams with determination and heart. With dedication and belief, you can achieve greatness and leave a lasting impact on the world.

ALEX MORGAN
The Icon of Determination

Under the bright lights of Old Trafford, the iconic stadium known as the Theatre of Dreams, Alex Morgan was about to carve her own legend in the annals of Olympic history. It was the 2012 London Olympic Games, and the U.S. Women's National Soccer Team was locked in a fierce battle against Canada in the semifinals—an intense match that would be remembered as one of the greatest in women's soccer.

The air was thick with anticipation as fans from around the world filled the stands, their cheers a vibrant tapestry of excitement and nerves. On the field, tension ran high. The game had been a rollercoaster, with the lead changing hands several times. As the clock ticked down, the score was tied 3-3, and the match seemed destined for penalties.

Alex, wearing her number 13 jersey, felt a mix of exhaustion and adrenaline as she looked around the field. Her teammates, equally weary, were depending on her, just as she depended on them. In the huddle before the start of extra time, Coach Pia Sundhage's words cut through the tension. "Stay focused, stay sharp. This is where legends are made," she said, her gaze locking with Alex's for a moment, instilling a deep sense of belief.

The first period of extra time passed without a goal, the intensity of the match not wavering for a second. As they moved into the second period, Alex's determination only intensified. She recalled the words of her father, Michael, who once told her, "In moments of pressure, champions rise." Holding onto that thought, she shook off the fatigue that clung to her limbs.

In the 123rd minute, just as the match seemed destined to end in a draw, a moment of magic unfolded. Megan Rapinoe, Alex's teammate known for her precise crosses, gained possession near the corner flag. Spotting Alex's quick movement towards the goal, Megan sent a soaring ball across the field. The stadium held its breath as the ball cut through the night sky.

Alex, timing her run perfectly, met the ball with a powerful header just six yards from the goal. The ball flew past the Canadian goalkeeper, the net billowing as the stadium erupted into deafening cheers. Alex's teammates rushed towards her, their faces a mixture of joy and disbelief. The U.S. team had taken a 4-3 lead, with mere seconds left on the clock.

Coach Sundhage's reaction was captured on the jumbotron, her arms thrown up in victory, a broad smile lighting up her face. "Alex did what she does best—deliver when it matters most," she later reflected in a post-match interview, her voice thick with pride.

In the stands, Alex's parents, Michael and Pamela, hugged each other tightly, tears of joy streaming down their faces. They had always believed in her, from those early days kicking a ball in their backyard to this monumental moment on the world stage.

The match ended with the U.S. securing their spot in the final, and Alex's goal was heralded as one of the most dramatic in Olympic history. It wasn't just the goal that made this moment legendary, but the resilience and teamwork displayed by the entire squad. In the final, the U.S. team clinched the gold medal by overcoming Japan with a 2-1 victory, avenging their defeat in the 2011 World Cup final decided by penalties.

Later, as Alex stood in the mixed zone, surrounded by reporters, she reflected on the significance of the victory. "This team never gives up. We push each other to the limit, and today, that belief carried us through," she said, her eyes gleaming with emotion.

Her rival from the Canadian team, Christine Sinclair, who had also played spectacularly that day, offered her thoughts as well. "Alex Morgan is a remarkable player. Today, she showed why she's one of the best in the world," Christine admitted with a respectful nod. This victory was more than just a win in a soccer match; it was a testament to Alex Morgan's spirit, her unwavering dedication, and her ability to rise to the occasion. From that day forward, Alex was not just a soccer player; she was a symbol of hope and a source of inspiration for millions, her legacy forever etched into the history of the sport.

As the celebrations continued and the crowd's roars echoed into the night, Alex knew this was a story she would tell for years to come—a story of determination, of dreams realized, and of a moment when she truly became a legend.

Early Life and Discovery of Talent

In the sunny, sprawling suburbs of Diamond Bar, California, a young girl named Alex Morgan kicked a soccer ball across her backyard with dreams as big as the sky above. Born to Michael and Pamela Morgan, who both had a passion for athletics, Alex was introduced to soccer at a tender age. From the beginning, her parents saw something special in her, a spark of greatness that could one day ignite into a brilliant flame.

As the sun rose over the Morgan family home, the rhythmic thump of a soccer ball echoed through the morning air. Michael, who had played college football, watched with a mixture of pride and nostalgia as his daughter dribbled and dashed across the grass. "You've got incredible talent, Alex!" he would exclaim, his voice booming across the yard, filled with excitement and encouragement.

Facing Early Challenges

Despite her innate skill and her parents' unwavering support, Alex faced numerous challenges on her path to soccer greatness. In her early days, she often found herself the only girl on all-boys teams, battling not just to score goals but to earn respect and acceptance in a male-dominated sport. Yet, on the field, gender barriers melted away as she showcased her speed, agility, and sharp soccer mind.

Alex's love for the game deepened with every practice and match. After school, she would race to the local park, her gear in tow, eager to meet her team and coach, Dan Flanagan, a veteran who had nurtured many young talents. "Alex is not just playing soccer; she lives it," Coach Flanagan would say to anyone who watched her play, his eyes twinkling with admiration. "She has the heart of a lioness."

Rising Star

The soccer field became Alex's haven, a place where she could express herself without words, communicating instead through swift passes and bold goals. Here, she felt truly alive, her earlier shyness transformed into a confident, commanding presence. Staring down the goal from midfield, she visualized her shots soaring past goalkeepers and into the net, each one bringing her closer to her dreams.

As Alex's skills sharpened, so did her reputation. By the time she reached high school, she was a known entity in California soccer circles, lauded for her perseverance and her leadership on and off the field. Her high school coach, Jenny Phillips, often highlighted Alex's unique blend of humility and intensity. "Alex leads by example. She's the first to arrive at practice and the last to leave. That dedication inspires the whole team," Coach Phillips would remark, her voice echoing with respect.

College Career and Professional Breakthrough

Success in high school led Alex to the University of California, Berkeley, where she not only dominated the collegiate soccer scene but also earned a degree in Political Economy. Her college coach, Neil McGuire, praised her academic and athletic balance. "Alex is a testament to what it means to be a student-athlete. She excels in both arenas because she understands the importance of discipline and focus," he observed, his words reflecting the pride he felt.

Alex's journey through college was marked by extraordinary victories and pivotal moments. Perhaps most memorable was her game-winning goal against the Stanford Cardinal, her team's fiercest rivals. The goal was not just a point on the scoreboard; it was a declaration of her arrival on the big stage, witnessed by scouts from the U.S. national team.

International Debut

Her transition to international play was seamless. Alex quickly became a vital player for the U.S. Women's National Team, her debut marked by a goal that would be the first of many. A rival from the Canadian National Team, Sophie Schmidt, once said, "Playing against Alex is like trying to catch smoke with your bare hands. She's elusive and always thinking one step ahead."

Coaches from around the world took note. Jill Ellis, the U.S. team coach during pivotal World Cups, often spoke of Alex's influence. "Alex brings more than just skill to our team; she brings a spirit that lifts everyone around her. Her ability to turn a game around with a single play is extraordinary," Coach Ellis would explain, her tone filled with admiration and respect.

Olympic Glory

One of Alex's most remarkable achievements came during the 2012 London Olympics, where she scored the game-winning goal in the semifinal against Canada in the 123rd minute—the latest goal ever scored in Olympic history. This victory not only demonstrated her physical and mental endurance but also cemented her status as a clutch performer on the world stage.

Off the field impact
Off the field, Alex's impact is just as profound. Through her foundation, she champions equal pay and better conditions for female athletes. Her teammates, like Megan Rapinoe, attest to her advocacy. "Alex uses her platform to fight for what's right, not just in soccer but in all sports. She's a role model for all of us," Megan stated, her voice earnest and fierce.

Final Reflections and Takeaway Messages
Alex Morgan continues to inspire, a shining example of how determination, passion, and love for what you do can lead to greatness. As she once said, "Dream big because dreams do happen." Her story is a reminder to all that with heart, hard work, and belief, anything is possible.

Key Takeaways from Alex Morgan's Story:

1. Dream Big and Start Early
Alex Morgan's journey began in her backyard, kicking a soccer ball with dreams as big as the sky. Her early start, combined with a passion for the game, set the foundation for her future success.
Takeaway: Start pursuing your dreams early and don't be afraid to dream big.

2. Overcome Challenges with Determination
Despite facing challenges like being the only girl on all-boys teams, Alex's determination and resilience shone through. She earned respect and acceptance

through her skills and hard work.
Takeaway: Overcome obstacles with determination and persistence, and let your actions speak for themselves.

3. Dedication Leads to Excellence
Alex's dedication to soccer was evident from her practice habits to her leadership on the field. Her high school and college coaches noted her exceptional work ethic and dedication.
Takeaway: Dedication and hard work are crucial to achieving excellence in any field.

4. Seize Opportunities and Rise to the Occasion
Alex's ability to perform under pressure, like scoring the game-winning goal in the 2012 London Olympics semifinal, highlights her capacity to rise to the occasion.
Takeaway: When opportunities arise, face them with confidence and give your best effort.

5. Embrace Teamwork and Inspire Others
Alex's journey emphasizes the importance of teamwork and supporting each other. Her leadership inspired her teammates, and together they achieved great victories.
Takeaway: Embrace teamwork, inspire those around you, and work towards common goals.

6. Balance Multiple Roles and Achieve Greatness
Balancing her athletic career with academics, Alex graduated from the University of California, Berkeley. Her success on and off the field showcases

her ability to excel in multiple areas.
Takeaway: Strive for balance and excel in various aspects of your life.

7. Stay Humble and Grateful

Despite her achievements, Alex remains humble and grateful, always acknowledging the support of her family, coaches, and teammates.
Takeaway: Stay humble, appreciate those who support you, and always give back.

8. Lead by Example and Inspire the Next Generation

Alex leads by example, showing that with heart, hard work, and belief, anything is possible. She inspires the next generation to pursue their dreams with courage and conviction.
Takeaway: Be a role model and inspire others through your actions and achievements.

Final Motivational Message

"Follow in Alex Morgan's footsteps—dream big, work hard, and never give up. Face challenges with determination, inspire others through your actions, and use your platform for good. Remember, with heart and belief, anything is possible. Dream big, because dreams do happen!"

RONALDINHO
"O Bruxo" (The Wizard)

Ronaldinho, born Ronaldo de Assis Moreira on March 21, 1980, in Porto Alegre, Brazil, grew up in a football-loving family. His father, João de Assis Moreira, worked as a shipyard worker and played football for a local club, instilling a deep love for the sport in young Ronaldinho. Tragically, Ronaldinho's father passed away when he was only eight years old, a loss that deeply affected him but also fueled his determination to succeed in football.

His mother, Dona Miguelina Elói Assis dos Santos, worked as a salesperson and later studied to become a nurse, demonstrating resilience and dedication to her family. Ronaldinho's older brother, Roberto, also played a significant role in his life. Roberto was a professional footballer whose career was cut short due to injury. Despite this setback, Roberto's influence and guidance were instrumental in Ronaldinho's development as a player.

Ronaldinho's love for football was evident from a young age. He spent countless hours playing on the streets and beaches of Porto Alegre, where he developed his unique style of play, characterized by creativity, flair, and an infectious joy. These early experiences laid the foundation for his extraordinary career and his ability to bring a sense of fun to the game.

Rising Through the Ranks

From a young age, Ronaldinho displayed extraordinary talent. At 13, he scored all 23 goals in a 23-0 victory for his local youth team, making headlines and drawing attention to his immense potential. This match, often referred to as the game that "introduced Ronaldinho to the world," highlighted his natural ability and passion for the sport.

In 1997, he was selected for Brazil's Under-17 national team and helped them win the FIFA Under-17 World Championship in Egypt, marking his arrival on the international stage. His performances in the tournament were nothing short of spectacular, showcasing his dribbling skills, vision, and goal-scoring prowess. This success was a crucial stepping stone in his career, as it brought him to the attention of scouts and clubs around the world.

Professional Career Beginnings

Ronaldinho began his professional career with Grêmio in Brazil, where his dazzling skills and creative play quickly made him a fan favorite. His success in the 1999 Copa Sul and Campeonato Gaúcho brought him into the limelight, paving the way for his move to Europe. At Grêmio, Ronaldinho was known for his ability to change the course of a game with a single moment of brilliance. His flair, combined with his work ethic, earned him respect from teammates and opponents alike.

One of the most memorable moments of his early

career came during the Rio Grande do Sul state championship, where he executed a stunning performance against Internacional, Grêmio's arch-rivals. Ronaldinho's dribbling and goal-scoring ability were on full display, earning him widespread acclaim and solidifying his status as a rising star in Brazilian football.

The Parisian Experience

In 2001, Ronaldinho signed with Paris Saint-Germain (PSG). His time in Paris was a period of growth and adaptation. Initially, he struggled to assert himself, often starting on the bench. However, his determination and dedication paid off as he honed his skills and became a key player for PSG. Despite the physical and aggressive nature of Ligue 1, Ronaldinho's talent shone through, and he left an indelible mark on the club.

During his time at PSG, Ronaldinho faced numerous challenges. The transition to European football was not easy, as he had to adapt to a different style of play and increased physicality. However, he used this period to refine his skills, particularly focusing on his fitness and tactical understanding of the game. His persistence paid off, and he soon became a fan favorite, known for his electrifying dribbles and spectacular goals.

One of the defining moments of his PSG career was his performance in the Coupe de la Ligue semi-final against Bordeaux. Ronaldinho scored a crucial goal and provided an assist, leading PSG to victory. Reflecting on his time in Paris, Ronaldinho said, "Paris was a learning experience. I grew as a player and as a person. The challenges I faced made me stronger and prepared me for the next steps in my career."

The Barcelona Years: A Golden Era
Ronaldinho's move to FC Barcelona in 2003 marked the beginning of the most successful phase of his career. His arrival at Camp Nou was transformative for the club. Under his influence, Barcelona won two La Liga titles, two Supercopas de España, and the UEFA Champions League. Ronaldinho's performances were nothing short of magical, earning him the FIFA World Player of the Year award in 2004 and 2005.

Ronaldinho's impact on Barcelona was immediate and profound. His style of play, characterized by technical brilliance and infectious joy, rejuvenated the team and brought back the glory days to Camp Nou. One of his most iconic moments came in the 2004-2005 season when he scored a breathtaking goal against Sevilla, dribbling past multiple defenders before unleashing a powerful shot that hit the crossbar and went in.

Another unforgettable moment was his performance against Real Madrid at the Santiago Bernabéu in 2005. Ronaldinho scored two stunning goals, leading Barcelona to a 3-0 victory and earning a standing ovation from the Real Madrid fans—a rare and extraordinary gesture. Reflecting on this moment, Ronaldinho said, "It was one of the most special nights of my career. To be applauded by the rival fans at the Bernabéu was a great honor."

During Ronaldinho's tenure at Barcelona, he played alongside a young Lionel Messi, who was beginning to make his mark on the football world. Ronaldinho played a crucial role in Messi's development, often providing guidance and support. The bond between the two players was evident on and off the pitch, and Ronaldinho's influence helped shape Messi into the player he would become. "Ronaldinho was a great mentor to me. He taught me so much about the game and about enjoying every moment on the field," Messi once said.

Challenges and Resilience

Ronaldinho's journey was not without its challenges. His last season at Barcelona was marred by injuries and a decline in form. The emergence of young talents like Lionel Messi meant Ronaldinho had to adapt and support the next generation. His move to AC Milan in 2008 provided a fresh start, and although he struggled initially, he eventually found his rhythm, leading Serie A in assists during the 2009-2010 season.

At AC Milan, Ronaldinho faced the challenge of proving himself once again. His first season was difficult, as he struggled with fitness and form. However, his resilience and determination saw him bounce back in the 2009-2010 season, where he played a pivotal role in Milan's success. Ronaldinho's ability to reinvent himself and continue performing at a high level was a testament to his character and dedication.

A Remarkable Defeat and Triumphant Revenge

One of the most remarkable defeats in Ronaldinho's career came during the 2006 UEFA Champions League final. Barcelona faced Arsenal, and despite Ronaldinho's best efforts, the team struggled in the first half, trailing 1-0. It was a moment of intense pressure and disappointment for the Brazilian star and his teammates. However, Barcelona managed to turn the game around in the second half, scoring two goals and winning the match 2-1. Although the victory was sweet, the struggle in the final was a humbling experience for Ronaldinho.

Seeking redemption, Ronaldinho was determined to lead his team to another Champions League triumph. In the 2005-2006 season, Barcelona faced Chelsea in the round of 16. The previous year, Chelsea had knocked Barcelona out of the competition, and this match was seen as an opportunity for revenge. Ronaldinho delivered a masterclass performance, scoring a stunning goal from the edge of the box and assisting another, leading Barcelona to a 2-1 victory and ultimately to the Champions League title. Reflecting on this victory, Ronaldinho said, "That win against Chelsea was about more than just advancing in the tournament. It was about showing our resilience and proving that we could overcome any obstacle."

Return to Brazil and Continued Success

In 2011, Ronaldinho returned to Brazil, signing with Flamengo and later Atlético Mineiro. His stint with Atlético Mineiro was particularly successful, leading them to their first Copa Libertadores title in 2013. Ronaldinho's ability to reinvent himself and continue to perform at a high level was inspirational to many young athletes.

At Atlético Mineiro, Ronaldinho became a beloved figure, both on and off the pitch. He led the team with his experience and skill, guiding them to their historic Copa Libertadores victory. His performance in the final against Olimpia was particularly memorable, as he orchestrated the team's attack and provided crucial assists. Reflecting on this period, Ronaldinho said, "Returning to Brazil and winning the Copa Libertadores was a dream come true. It was a reward for all the hard work and sacrifices."

International Glory

Ronaldinho's international career was equally illustrious. He was a pivotal figure in Brazil's 2002 FIFA World Cup victory, famously scoring a memorable free-kick against England in the quarter-finals. He also played a significant role in Brazil's Copa America wins in 1999 and 2004, and the FIFA Confederations Cup victory in 2005.

One of Ronaldinho's most memorable international moments came during the 2002 World Cup quarter-final against England. With the match tied at 1-1, Ronaldinho took a free-kick from 40 yards out, lofting the ball over the England goalkeeper David Seaman and into the net. This goal not only secured Brazil's place in the semi-finals but also highlighted Ronaldinho's genius and creativity. Reflecting on this moment, he said, "That goal against England was one of the most important of my career. It was a combination of instinct and skill."

Final Reflections and Takeaway Message

Ronaldinho's influence on football goes beyond numbers and trophies. Reflecting on his career, he said, "Football is about joy. I've always played with a smile because when you love what you do, you can achieve great things." His electrifying style, marked by creativity, flair, and an infectious joy, captivated millions worldwide. Ronaldinho made the game more entertaining with iconic moves like the "elastico" and no-look passes, leaving an unforgettable mark on the sport and inspiring fans across the globe.

Ronaldinho's story teaches us several key lessons:

1. Embrace Joy and Passion

Ronaldinho always played with a smile, showing that enjoying the process is as important as the results.

Takeaway: Find joy in what you do. Passion and enjoyment in your work can lead to great achievements and a fulfilling career.

2. Resilience and Adaptability: Ronaldinho faced many challenges, from personal loss to professional setbacks, but he continually adapted and persevered.

Takeaway: Embrace resilience and adaptability. Overcoming challenges and adapting to new situations is essential for long-term success.

3. Mentorship and Teamwork: His support for young talents like Lionel Messi highlights the importance of helping others grow while achieving personal success.

Takeaway: Support and mentor others. Teamwork and helping others grow can enhance your own success and create a positive impact on those around you.

4. Dedication and Hard Work: Ronaldinho's success was built on years of dedication and relentless pursuit of excellence.

Takeaway: Dedication and hard work are crucial. Consistent effort and a commitment to excellence are the foundations of achieving your goals.

5. Overcoming Adversity
His career is a testament to overcoming obstacles and turning defeats into opportunities for growth and success.
Takeaway: Turn adversity into opportunity. Use setbacks as a chance to grow and learn, transforming challenges into stepping stones for future success.

Final Motivational Message

Ronaldinho's journey from the streets of Porto Alegre to the pinnacle of world football is a testament to his extraordinary talent, resilience, and love for the game. His story is a powerful reminder that with hard work, dedication, and a positive attitude, anything is possible. For young aspiring athletes, Ronaldinho's career serves as an enduring source of inspiration, illustrating that true greatness comes from a combination of skill, joy, and relentless perseverance. As you pursue your dreams, remember Ronaldinho's words: "You should be proud of what you do. When you love what you do, you can touch the sky." Let his journey inspire you to embrace every challenge, find joy in your passions, and strive for excellence in all that you do. With determination and a smile, you too can achieve greatness and make a lasting impact on the world.

MARTA

The Queen of Soccer

In the small town of Dois Riachos, Brazil, a young girl named Marta Vieira da Silva discovered her passion for soccer. Born to a single mother who worked tirelessly to support her family, Marta's early life was marked by hardship and struggle. Yet, amidst the challenges, she found solace and joy in the simple act of kicking a ball.

Marta's love for soccer began on the dusty streets of her neighborhood, where she played with the boys, often being the only girl on the field. Her talent was evident from a young age, as she effortlessly dribbled past older and stronger opponents. Despite the societal norms and expectations placed upon her, Marta's mother, Dona Tereza, always supported her dream. "You were born to play, Marta," she would say, her voice filled with unwavering belief and encouragement.

Overcoming Obstacles

As Marta grew older, her talent became impossible to ignore. However, her journey was far from easy. The world of soccer, especially in Brazil, was heavily dominated by men, and opportunities for girls were scarce. Marta faced discrimination and ridicule, but her determination never wavered. "Soccer is not just a game for me," she would say. "It's my way of life, and I won't let anyone take that away from me."

At the age of 14, Marta's talent caught the attention of Helena Pacheco, a coach for the Vasco da Gama women's team. Helena saw the raw potential in Marta and invited her to join the team in Rio de Janeiro. This was a turning point in Marta's life, as it meant leaving her family and hometown behind to pursue her dream. With a heavy heart but determined spirit, Marta embarked on this new chapter.

Early Career and Setbacks

Life in Rio was challenging. Marta was far from home, and the demands of professional training were grueling. She often felt the pangs of homesickness and the weight of expectations. Yet, her love for the game kept her going. "Every time I step on the field, I remember why I started playing," Marta would say, her eyes reflecting her unyielding resolve.

Marta's early career was marked by both triumphs and setbacks. She quickly became a standout player for Vasco da Gama, but the team faced financial difficulties, and the women's program was eventually disbanded. Undeterred, Marta moved to the Santa Cruz club, where she continued to hone her skills and attract attention from national selectors.

Breakthrough and International Stardom

Marta's big break came when she was called up to the Brazilian national team. Her debut at the 2003 Women's World Cup in the United States marked the beginning of her rise to international stardom. Despite

Brazil not winning the tournament, Marta's exceptional performance caught the eye of scouts from around the world.

In 2004, Marta joined Umeå IK in Sweden, a move that would elevate her career to new heights. The transition to European soccer was not without challenges. Marta had to adapt to a different style of play and a new culture. "It was tough at first," she recalled in an interview. "But I knew this was my opportunity to prove myself on the world stage."

Moments of Glory and Heartbreak

Marta's time at Umeå IK was marked by incredible success. She led the team to multiple league titles and was named the FIFA World Player of the Year in 2006, the first of many such accolades. Yet, her journey was also filled with moments of heartbreak.

One of the most poignant moments came at the 2007 Women's World Cup in China. Brazil reached the final, and Marta, the tournament's top scorer, was expected to lead her team to victory. However, Brazil lost to Germany, and Marta missed a crucial penalty. The defeat was devastating, but Marta's response was a testament to her character. "We win together, and we lose together," she said, tears in her eyes. "This loss will make us stronger."

Marta's teammate, Cristiane, also spoke about her influence on the team. "Marta's passion and drive are contagious. She lifts us all up, especially in the toughest moments," Cristiane said. "Her resilience is something we all admire and strive to emulate."

The Ultimate Defeat and Glorious Revenge

The 2008 Beijing Olympics presented another significant challenge for Marta and the Brazilian team. They advanced to the final, facing the United States in a highly anticipated match. Despite their best efforts, Brazil lost 1-0 in extra time, a heartbreaking defeat for Marta, who had once again carried her team through the tournament with exceptional performances.

This loss weighed heavily on Marta. "It was one of the hardest moments of my career," she later admitted. "But I knew we had to come back stronger."

The opportunity for redemption came at the 2011 Women's World Cup in Germany. Brazil and the United States met again, this time in the quarterfinals. The match was a thrilling battle, with both teams displaying remarkable skill and determination. In the dying moments of extra time, with the score tied 2-2, Marta delivered a stunning assist to her teammate, sending Brazil through to the semifinals.

Unyielding Determination

Despite the setbacks, Marta's determination never waned. She continued to push herself, both physically and mentally, striving to become the best player in the world. Her relentless work ethic and passion for the game inspired her teammates and young players around the globe. "Marta's dedication is unmatched," said her long-time coach, Doriva Bueno. "She trains harder than anyone, always looking to improve."

Marta's rivals also recognized her extraordinary talent and spirit. Abby Wambach, a star player for the United States, once remarked, "Marta is one of the fiercest competitors I've ever faced. Her ability to change the game in an instant is incredible. She inspires not just her team, but everyone who loves soccer."

Inspirational Achievements

Marta's career is filled with countless achievements that serve as inspiration for young athletes. She has won six FIFA World Player of the Year awards, more than any other player, male or female. She is the all-time leading scorer in Women's World Cup history, a record that speaks to her enduring excellence on the global stage.

One of the most inspiring moments in Marta's career came during the 2019 Women's World Cup in France. Brazil faced a tough match against Italy, and Marta delivered a stirring speech to her teammates before the game. "We are here to make history," she said. "Play with heart, play for each other, and never give up." Brazil won the match, and Marta's leadership and passion were pivotal.

Extraordinary Victories

Marta's career has been marked by numerous extraordinary victories that highlight her skill and determination. One of her most memorable performances was during the 2007 Women's World Cup quarterfinal against the United States. Marta scored two stunning goals, leading Brazil to a 4-0 victory. Her second goal, a dazzling solo effort, left the American defense in disarray and is still considered one of the greatest goals in Women's World Cup history. "Marta was unstoppable that day," said Abby Wambach. "She showed the world what true greatness looks like."

Another remarkable achievement was her

performance in the 2008 Olympic Games in Beijing. Marta led Brazil to the final, where they faced the United States. Although Brazil lost in extra time, Marta's skill and determination were on full display throughout the tournament. "Marta played with incredible heart and skill," said Pia Sundhage, the coach of the U.S. team. "She is a player who can change the course of a game with a single moment of brilliance."

Giving Back and Legacy

Off the field, Marta has used her platform to advocate for gender equality in sports and society. She has spoken out about the disparities in resources and opportunities for women in soccer and has worked to empower young girls to pursue their dreams. "I want to leave a legacy of hope and possibility," Marta said in an interview. "If I can inspire even one girl to believe in herself, then all the struggles and sacrifices will be worth it."

Marta's foundation, the Marta Vieira da Silva Institute, focuses on providing educational and athletic opportunities for underprivileged children in Brazil. Through her foundation, Marta aims to give back to the community that supported her and to create pathways for the next generation of athletes. "I want to give children the chance to dream big, just like I did," Marta explained. "Everyone deserves the opportunity to chase their dreams."

Final Reflections and Takeaway Message

Marta's journey from a small town in Brazil to becoming a global soccer icon is filled with valuable lessons that can inspire young readers to pursue their dreams with determination and passion.

Key Takeaways from Marta's Story:

1. Embrace Your Passion
From a young age, Marta found joy and purpose in playing soccer. She never let societal norms or expectations deter her from pursuing what she loved.
Takeaway: Find your passion and embrace it wholeheartedly. Let it guide you and bring joy to your life.

2. Overcome Obstacles with Determination
Marta faced numerous challenges, from financial hardships to discrimination. Despite these obstacles, she remained focused and determined.
Takeaway: Life will throw challenges your way, but your determination will help you overcome them. Never give up, no matter how tough the journey gets.

3. Believe in Yourself
Even when others doubted her abilities, Marta believed in herself and her potential.
Takeaway: Self-belief is a powerful tool. Trust in your abilities and have confidence in your journey. You are capable of achieving greatness.

4. Learn from Setbacks
Marta experienced significant defeats, such as the loss at the 2008 Beijing Olympics. Instead of being

discouraged, she used these moments to fuel her drive for success.
Takeaway: Setbacks are opportunities for growth. Learn from them, and let them make you stronger and more resilient.

5. Lead with Heart and Inspire Others
Marta's leadership on and off the field has inspired countless young athletes. Her speeches and actions motivated her teammates and fans alike.
Takeaway: Lead with your heart and inspire those around you. Your passion and dedication can have a profound impact on others.

6. Give Back to Your Community
Marta's work through her foundation highlights the importance of giving back and creating opportunities for others.
Takeaway: Use your success to help others. Giving back to your community enriches your life and creates a positive legacy.

Final Motivational Message
Marta's story is a powerful reminder that dreams are achievable with hard work, resilience, and unwavering self-belief. She faced countless challenges and setbacks but never lost sight of her goals. Her journey teaches us that greatness is not just about personal achievements but also about inspiring and uplifting others.
"Remember, there are no limits to what you can achieve. Embrace your passions, overcome your obstacles, believe in yourself, and inspire those around

you. Your journey is unique and filled with endless possibilities. Keep dreaming big and chasing your goals with all your heart. The future is yours to create."- Marta Vieira da Silva

Let Marta's story be a beacon of hope and inspiration, encouraging you to pursue your dreams and make a difference in the world.

ZINEDINE ZIDANE
The Maestro of Elegance

The scene was set at Hampden Park in Glasgow, Scotland, on a warm May evening in 2002. The atmosphere was electric, with over 50,000 fervent fans filling the stadium, their cheers echoing through the night. This was the UEFA Champions League final, a clash between Real Madrid and Bayer Leverkusen. It was more than just a game; it was a battle of skill, pride, and honor.

Real Madrid needed a victory to reaffirm their dominance in European football, but Bayer Leverkusen, driven by their underdog spirit, were equally determined to make history. The tension was palpable as the players lined up, the weight of expectation pressing down on their shoulders.

As the match began, both teams displayed relentless intensity. Tackles flew in, and the game ebbed and flowed with breathtaking speed. The first half saw goals from both sides, ending 1-1. Zinedine Zidane, as always, was at the heart of Real Madrid's attack, orchestrating play with his elegant touches and visionary passes.

But it was in the final moments of the first half that the legend of Zinedine Zidane reached its zenith. With the score tied and the first half nearing its end, Real Madrid launched one final attack. Roberto Carlos sprinted down the left wing, delivering a high cross into the box. Zidane, positioned perfectly, watched the ball descend, and with a moment of pure brilliance, he executed a sublime left-footed volley that soared into the top corner of the net. The stadium erupted in jubilation as Zidane ran towards the corner flag, his face a mask of triumph and relief. His teammates swarmed him, their joy palpable.

That night, Zidane not only secured a crucial victory for Real Madrid but also etched his name into the annals of football history. The image of his majestic volley became an iconic symbol of his elegance and skill. "This is why he's the best," remarked Raúl, Zidane's teammate, with admiration. "In moments of great pressure, Zidane delivers."

Early Life and Discovery of Talent

In the bustling city of Marseille, France, Zinedine Yazid Zidane was born on June 23, 1972, to Smaïl and Malika Zidane. From a very early age, it was clear that Zinedine, or "Zizou" as he was affectionately called, was no ordinary child. He displayed an exceptional talent for football that set him apart from his peers. This talent was nurtured in a family that, despite their modest means, was deeply supportive of his passion. Zidane's father, Smaïl, worked as a warehouseman, while his mother, Malika, was a homemaker. Despite their modest means, the Zidane family was close-knit and supportive of Zinedine's dreams. Smaïl often took Zinedine to training sessions and matches, encouraging him with words of pride and hope.

By the age of five, Zidane was playing for a local youth

team, where his elegant style and raw talent quickly stood out. "One day, the whole world will know your name," his mother would say, her words carrying the conviction that only a loving parent could provide.

The Struggles Begin

Despite his prodigious talent, Zidane faced significant challenges. Growing up in the tough neighborhood of La Castellane, he often had to navigate a path fraught with difficulties. His competitive nature and refined style of play, while effective, sometimes clashed with the rough-and-tumble approach of street football.

At the age of 14, Zidane was scouted by AS Cannes, marking the beginning of a new chapter in his life. Moving away from home to join the Cannes academy, Zidane found himself in a new environment, one filled with both opportunity and new challenges.

Rising Through the Ranks

Joining the AS Cannes academy, Zidane quickly adapted to his new surroundings. The transition was challenging, but his relentless work ethic and natural talent shone through. He excelled on the field, becoming one of the top prospects in French football.

From the outset, Zidane's talent was evident. He quickly moved up through the ranks, impressing everyone with his vision, technique, and calm demeanor. Yet, it was not just his talent that set him apart but also his relentless work ethic. "Talent without hard work is nothing," Zidane would often say, echoing the words of his father.

His coach at Cannes, Jean Varraud, once said, "Zinedine was always the first to arrive and the last to leave. His dedication was unmatched, and his passion for the game was evident in every training session."

Breakthrough and Early Success

Zidane's breakthrough came in 1989 when he made his debut for the AS Cannes senior team at just 17 years old. His initial appearances were marked by flashes of brilliance, and it was clear that a star was in the making. However, the path to stardom was not without its setbacks. Injuries and the pressure of performing at a high level tested his resilience and determination.

Despite these obstacles, Zidane's resolve never wavered. His dedication to recovery and improvement was unwavering. "Every setback is an opportunity to come back stronger," he would say, his eyes reflecting the steely determination that had become his trademark.

The Era of Dominance

By the mid-1990s, Zidane had established himself as a key player for both club and country. His performances for Bordeaux and later Juventus were nothing short of spectacular, earning him accolades and respect from teammates and opponents alike.

Teammates and opponents alike marveled at his skills. Alessandro Del Piero, a legendary forward at Juventus, once said, "Playing alongside Zinedine is like playing with the best player in the playground. You give him the ball, and you know something magical will happen."

The Words of Coaches and Teammates

Marcello Lippi, who coached Zidane during some of his

most prolific years at Juventus, once remarked, "Zidane is the best player I have ever seen. The difference between him and the others is his mindset. He is always looking to improve, never satisfied with what he has achieved."

Teammate Didier Deschamps shared a similar sentiment, "Training with Zinedine is an honor. He pushes everyone to be better. His humility and work ethic are what make him truly great."

A Remarkable Defeat and Redemption

While Zidane's career has been filled with numerous triumphs, it has also seen significant defeats. One of the most memorable was the 2006 FIFA World Cup final against Italy. Despite scoring a penalty in the first half, Zidane was sent off in extra time for a retaliatory foul against Marco Materazzi. The match ended in a penalty shootout, with Italy emerging victorious. The defeat was particularly painful as it was Zidane's final game before retirement. "It was one of the hardest moments of my career," he admitted in an interview. "But such moments make you stronger."

The following year, Zidane transitioned into coaching, determined to achieve success off the field. In 2016, he was appointed head coach of Real Madrid. His tenure saw remarkable success, including winning three consecutive UEFA Champions League titles. The victories were a testament to his tenacity and leadership. "We learned from our defeats," Zidane reflected. "They made us stronger and more united."

The Struggles of the National Team

While Zidane's club career soared, success with the French national team was more challenging. Despite his best efforts, the team faced criticism and doubt from the media and fans. The weight of expectations was immense, and the pressure took a toll on Zidane. In 2006, after the World Cup final, Zidane announced his retirement from professional football. The decision was met with mixed emotions. "I've given everything I have to this sport," he said, his voice heavy with emotion. "It's time to step aside and let the next generation carry the torch."

A New Chapter of Leadership

After retiring from playing, Zinedine Zidane's influence on football only grew stronger as he transitioned into coaching. His passion for the sport remained undiminished, leading Real Madrid to unprecedented success. In 2020, his perseverance and dedication were recognized when he was named FIFA Best Men's Coach, a testament to his resilience and belief in the power of football. "Never give up on your dreams, no matter how difficult the journey may be," Zidane said with emotion.

Real Madrid's president, Florentino Pérez, highlighted Zidane's impact, stating, "Having Zinedine as our coach is a blessing. His presence lifts the entire team, and his commitment to excellence is infectious. He continues to set the standard for what it means to be a professional footballer." Zidane's journey from player to coach exemplifies his unwavering pursuit of excellence and his enduring influence on the game.

Extraordinary Victories and Records

Zidane's career has been marked by extraordinary victories and record-breaking performances. One of the most memorable moments came in 1998 when he scored two headers in the World Cup final, leading France to victory. His ability to perform at the highest level consistently earned him the admiration of fans and respect from peers worldwide.

Another highlight was the 2000 UEFA European Championship, where Zidane's brilliance helped France secure the title. Thierry Henry, a key member of that team, said, "Zizou's presence on the pitch lifts everyone's game. He makes us all believe that anything is possible."

Final Reflections and Takeaway Message

Zinedine Zidane's career exemplifies perseverance, hard work, and self-belief. From his early days in Marseille to global stardom, his journey teaches young athletes that success comes from overcoming challenges. Beyond football, Zidane's humility shines through his foundation work, helping underprivileged children. "I want to give back to the community that has given me so much," he says. Widely admired, even Pelé once said, "Zidane makes me proud." His story continues to inspire future generations to dream big, work hard, and persevere, as Zidane reminds us, "You have to fight for your dream."

Zidane's story teaches us several key lessons:

1. The Power of Determination
In 2002, during a crucial Champions League final, Zidane's determination led to a game-winning goal, solidifying his legendary status and demonstrating that resilience can lead to extraordinary achievements.

Takeaway: Never give up, even when the situation seems impossible.

2. Support from Loved Ones
Zidane's talent was nurtured by his supportive family, especially his father and mother, despite financial difficulties.
Takeaway: Surround yourself with people who believe in you.

3. Overcoming Adversity
Growing up in a tough neighborhood and facing early career challenges, Zidane continued his dream with unwavering determination.
Takeaway: Face challenges head-on and stay hopeful.

4. Hard Work and Dedication
Zidane's relentless hard work and dedication led him to become one of the world's best, despite early struggles and setbacks.
Takeaway: Talent is important, but hard work and dedication make the difference.

5. Learning from Defeat
After a painful loss in the 2006 World Cup final, Zidane used the experience to come back stronger, demonstrating the importance of learning from setbacks.
Takeaway: Every defeat is an opportunity to learn and grow.

6. National Team Perseverance

Despite challenges and criticism, Zidane persisted with the French national team and eventually led them to win major titles.
Takeaway: Persistence pays off.

7. Continual Pursuit of Excellence
Even after achieving success, Zidane sought new challenges in coaching, making an immediate impact. *Takeaway: Never stop striving for excellence.*

8. Giving Back
Through his foundation, Zidane provides opportunities for underprivileged children in education, healthcare, and sports.
Takeaway: Use your success to help others.

Final Motivational Message
Zinedine Zidane's journey from a young boy in Marseille to a football legend is a powerful reminder that with determination, hard work, and the support of loved ones, any dream is achievable. His story encourages us all to fight for our dreams, remain resilient in the face of adversity, and give back to others. No matter where you start, your journey can inspire countless others if you dare to dream big and work tirelessly to make those dreams a reality.

ZLATAN IBRAHIMOVIĆ
The Lion of the Pitch

I n the gritty streets of Malmö, Sweden, a young boy named Zlatan Ibrahimović was kicking a tattered football around with fierce determination. Born on October 3, 1981, to a Bosnian father and a Croatian mother, Zlatan's childhood was far from easy. Poverty, instability, and the harsh realities of life in the immigrant-dominated district of Rosengård shaped his early years. But it was on these rough streets that Zlatan's remarkable journey to football greatness began.

Childhood Struggles and Early Passion for Football

Growing up in Rosengård, Zlatan faced numerous challenges. His family struggled to make ends meet, and the environment was far from conducive to nurturing young talent. Yet, amidst these difficulties, Zlatan found solace and purpose in football. The local pitch became his sanctuary, a place where he could escape the hardships of daily life.

"Football was my release, my escape," Zlatan recalls. "Whenever I had the ball at my feet, nothing else mattered. I was free."

His talent was undeniable from an early age. Coaches and peers alike were astonished by his natural ability, his flair, and his unyielding confidence. However, Zlatan's road to professional football was not smooth. He was often misunderstood, seen as brash and arrogant. But those close to him knew that beneath the tough exterior was a young boy with a burning desire to prove himself.

The Breakthrough: Malmö FF

Zlatan's big break came when he joined the youth academy of Malmö FF, one of Sweden's most prestigious football clubs. Here, he honed his skills and began to attract attention for his extraordinary talent. But it wasn't just his skills that set him apart—it was his attitude, his unshakeable belief in his own abilities. One of his early coaches, Johnny Gyllensjö, saw something special in him. "Zlatan was different," Gyllensjö said in an interview. "He had this swagger, this confidence that was beyond his years. He wasn't just playing the game; he was owning it."

Despite his talent, Zlatan's journey was not without setbacks. There were moments of frustration, times when his temper got the better of him, and instances when he felt the weight of expectations crushing down. Yet, he never wavered in his pursuit of greatness.

Rise to Stardom: Ajax and Juventus

In 2001, Zlatan made a significant move to Ajax, a club renowned for its youth development. This transition marked the beginning of his rise to international stardom. At Ajax, he continued to dazzle with his skills, scoring spectacular goals and leading the team to several victories. However, his time at Ajax was also marked by controversy, including a well-publicized clash with teammate Rafael van der Vaart.

"I was never afraid to speak my mind," Zlatan later reflected. "Some people didn't like that, but I wasn't there to make friends. I was there to win."

From Ajax, Zlatan's journey took him to Juventus in 2004. His time in Italy was transformative. Under the tutelage of coach Fabio Capello, Zlatan refined his game, becoming more disciplined and tactically aware. Capello recognized Zlatan's potential and pushed him to his limits.

"Capello was tough, but he made me a better player," Zlatan said. "He taught me the importance of hard work and discipline."

Triumphs and Tribulations: Inter Milan and Barcelona

Zlatan's career continued to soar as he moved to Inter Milan in 2006. At Inter, he became the focal point of the team's attack, winning three consecutive Serie A titles. However, his career was not without its difficulties. In 2009, Zlatan transferred to Barcelona, a move that many thought would be the pinnacle of his career. Yet, his time at Barcelona was marred by clashes with coach Pep Guardiola and struggles to fit into the team's style of play.

"At Barcelona, I felt like I was being held back," Zlatan said in his autobiography. "Guardiola wanted me to play a certain way, but I needed to be free, to express myself."

Despite the challenges, Zlatan's determination never

faltered. He moved to AC Milan in 2010, where he once again showcased his brilliance, leading the team to a Serie A title and proving that he was still one of the best in the world.

The Parisian Dream: Paris Saint-Germain

In 2012, Zlatan embarked on a new adventure with Paris Saint-Germain (PSG). His impact was immediate and profound. Zlatan's time at PSG was characterized by spectacular goals, numerous titles, and a reinvention of his image. He became a leader, a mentor to younger players, and a symbol of the club's ambition.

"I came to Paris to create history," Zlatan declared. "And we did."

His time at PSG solidified his legacy as one of the greatest footballers of his generation. He won multiple Ligue 1 titles and became the club's all-time leading scorer. Yet, it wasn't just his on-field achievements that defined him—it was his larger-than-life personality, his quotable remarks, and his unwavering confidence.

A Remarkable Defeat and the Sweet Taste of Revenge

Zlatan's journey is marked not just by triumphs but also by remarkable defeats followed by sweet revenge. One of the most notable instances occurred during his time at Manchester United. In the 2016-17 season, United faced a devastating defeat against their fierce rivals, Manchester City, losing 2-1 at Old Trafford. The loss was a blow to Zlatan, who had always thrived in big matches.

However, true to his resilient nature, Zlatan used this defeat as fuel for his determination. In the return fixture at the Etihad Stadium, Zlatan played a crucial role in United's 2-0 victory, notching a goal and leading by example. The victory was not just a win on the scoreboard but a statement of his relentless spirit and ability to bounce back from setbacks.

Later Years: Manchester United and LA Galaxy

Even as he approached the twilight of his career, Zlatan continued to defy expectations. In 2016, he joined Manchester United, where he played a pivotal role in winning the Europa League and the League Cup. Despite a serious knee injury in 2017, Zlatan made a remarkable comeback, proving that age and setbacks could not diminish his drive or talent.

José Mourinho, his coach at Manchester United, admired his resilience. "Zlatan is a warrior," Mourinho said. "He came back from a serious injury and still performed at the highest level. His mentality is extraordinary."

In 2018, Zlatan moved to the LA Galaxy in Major League Soccer (MLS), where he once again became a sensation. His time in the United States was marked by breathtaking performances and memorable quotes, including his famous statement, "I came, I saw, I conquered."

A Return to Milan and Legacy

In a fitting turn of events, Zlatan returned to AC Milan in 2020. His presence revitalized the team, and even in his late 30s, he continued to score goals and lead by example. Stefano Pioli, the AC Milan coach, praised

Zlatan's influence on the team. "Zlatan brings a winning mentality," Pioli said. "He pushes everyone to be their best."

His career, spanning over two decades, became a testament to his resilience, adaptability, and relentless pursuit of excellence.

Inspirational Messages and Quotes

Throughout his career, Zlatan Ibrahimović has inspired countless young athletes with his words and actions. His journey from the streets of Malmö to the grandest stages of football is a powerful reminder of what can be achieved with hard work, self-belief, and an unyielding spirit.

"Always believe in yourself," Zlatan often says. "No matter what others think, if you have a dream, you must protect it. And you must be willing to fight for it."

His coaches and teammates have also shared stories that highlight Zlatan's incredible work ethic and determination.

"Zlatan is the hardest worker I've ever seen," said his former PSG coach Laurent Blanc. "He never settles for less than perfection."

Thiago Silva, his teammate at PSG, once remarked, "Zlatan taught us to always aim higher. He pushed everyone to be better, and he led by example."

Final Reflections and Takeaway Message

Zlatan Ibrahimović's story is one of triumph over adversity, relentless pursuit of greatness, and unwavering self-belief. From his humble beginnings in Rosengård to becoming a global football icon, Zlatan's journey inspires young athletes worldwide. His legacy goes beyond titles and goals, serving as a beacon of hope for those who dare to dream big. Zlatan's story reminds us that no dream is too big, no challenge too great, and no goal unattainable if pursued with courage and determination. His life exemplifies that greatness comes from hard work, resilience, and belief in oneself.

Ibrahimović's story teaches us several key lessons:

1. Embrace Your Passion

Zlatan Ibrahimović found solace and purpose in football from a young age. His love for the game drove him through tough times and shaped his future.

Takeaway: Find what you love and let it be your driving force.

2. Believe in Yourself

Zlatan's unshakeable confidence in his abilities set him apart, even when others doubted him. His self-belief was a cornerstone of his success.

Takeaway: Believe in yourself, even when others don't.

3. Overcome Adversity

Growing up in poverty and facing numerous challenges, Zlatan turned his hardships into motivation to succeed.

Takeaway: Turn obstacles into opportunities to grow stronger and more determined.

4. Work Hard

Behind every victory were hours of hard work and

discipline. Coaches and teammates have praised Zlatan's incredible work ethic.
Takeaway: Success doesn't come easy—work hard and stay disciplined.

5. Learn from Setbacks
Zlatan faced significant defeats and challenges, including injuries and conflicts. Instead of giving up, he used these setbacks to come back stronger.
Takeaway: Learn from your setbacks and use them to fuel your comeback.

6. Stay True to Yourself
Throughout his career, Zlatan remained true to his personality and style, never compromising his essence to fit others' expectations.
Takeaway: Be authentic and stay true to who you are.

7. Aim for Greatness
Zlatan always aimed for the top, striving for excellence in every team he played for.
Takeaway: Set high goals for yourself and strive for excellence in everything you do.

8. Inspiration to Others
Zlatan's journey from the streets of Malmö to becoming a football legend inspires countless young athletes to pursue their dreams with relentless determination.
Takeaway: Let your journey inspire others.

9. Family Support and Humility

Despite his confidence and success, Zlatan credits his family's support and emphasizes the importance of humility and dedication.

Takeaway: Stay humble and appreciate those who support you.

Final Motivational Message

Zlatan Ibrahimović's story is a testament to the power of dreams and unwavering self-belief. His journey shows that no dream is too big and no challenge too great if pursued with courage and determination. As Zlatan famously said, "I am not like you. I am Zlatan. And if I can do it, so can you."

Greatness isn't just about talent—it's about hard work, resilience, and staying true to yourself. No matter your background or obstacles, you have the potential to achieve incredible things. The road to success may be tough, but with determination, you can reach heights you never imagined.

Lace up your boots, step onto your field of dreams, and remember: the only limits are the ones you set for yourself. Your journey to greatness starts now—embrace it with all your heart.

MEGAN RAPINOE
The Trailblazer of Courage

In the summer of 2019, the world turned its eyes to France, where the FIFA Women's World Cup was underway. Among the many talented players, Megan Rapinoe stood out, not just for her vibrant pink hair and confident demeanor but for her unparalleled skill and determination. It was in this tournament that Megan would etch her name into the annals of soccer history with a performance that exemplified her status as a true legend of the sport.

The Quarterfinal Against France
The stage was set for a dramatic encounter in the quarterfinals as the U.S. Women's National Team faced the host nation, France. The pressure was immense, with the eyes of millions watching. France, a formidable opponent, had the advantage of home support, and the match was billed as the clash of titans. Megan knew the significance of this game. "This is where legends are made," she told her teammates in the locker room, her voice steady and filled with conviction.

From the first whistle, the intensity of the game was palpable. The French team pressed hard, determined to make their home advantage count. However, Megan was undeterred. In the fifth minute, a free-kick was awarded to the U.S. team. Stepping up with her trademark calmness, Megan struck the ball with precision. It soared over the wall of French defenders and curled into the net, past the outstretched hands of the goalkeeper. The stadium erupted, but it was the American fans whose cheers echoed the loudest.

Megan's Leadership on Display

As the game progressed, Megan's leadership was evident in every play. She directed her teammates, encouraged them, and led by example. "Megan is not just a player; she's a commander on the field," remarked her coach, Jill Ellis, during a post-match interview. Her influence was undeniable, as she orchestrated the team's movements and maintained their composure under relentless French attacks.

Despite the early lead, the French team was relentless, pushing forward with every opportunity. The U.S. defense was tested repeatedly, but Megan's presence provided a calming influence. Her strategic positioning and timely interventions disrupted French advances, showcasing her defensive prowess as well as her attacking capabilities.

The Second Goal and Iconic Celebration

The second half saw the French team intensify their efforts to equalize. The U.S. team, however, remained resolute. In the 65th minute, Megan found herself in the perfect position again. A swift counter-attack saw her racing down the left flank. Receiving a precise pass from Tobin Heath, Megan controlled the ball deftly and, with a powerful strike, sent it crashing into the back of the net. The score was now 2-0.

What followed was one of the most iconic moments in sports history. Megan sprinted towards the corner flag, stopped, and stood with arms outstretched, soaking in the adulation. It was a pose of triumph and defiance, encapsulating her spirit. "That celebration was a statement," she later explained. "It was about owning the moment and showing the world what we're made of."

An Inspirational Journey

In the small town of Redding, California, a young girl named Megan Rapinoe discovered her love for soccer. Born to a family that cherished sports, Megan found herself drawn to the soccer field, where she could express herself freely. Her journey from a spirited child with big dreams to an internationally celebrated athlete is a story of resilience, determination, and an unwavering belief in oneself.

Childhood and Early Beginnings

Megan Rapinoe was born on July 5, 1985, to Jim and Denise Rapinoe. The youngest of six siblings, Megan grew up in a household where sports were a significant part of life. Her older brother, Brian, was her biggest influence. Despite Brian's struggles with substance abuse, his passion for sports inspired Megan. She often credits him for her early interest in soccer, saying, "Brian was my hero. He was always so talented, and I wanted to be just like him."

At the age of five, Megan and her fraternal twin sister, Rachael, joined a local soccer team. From the moment she stepped onto the field, it was clear that Megan had found her calling. Her parents noticed her natural talent and relentless energy, nurturing her passion with unwavering support. Denise Rapinoe often recalled, "Megan had this spark in her eyes when she played. We knew she was destined for greatness."

Overcoming Adversity

Megan's journey was not without challenges. Growing up, she faced the heartbreak of seeing her brother struggle with addiction and frequent incarcerations. These experiences had a profound impact on her, teaching her the importance of resilience and mental toughness. "Watching Brian go through what he did was incredibly hard," Megan recalled. "But it also made me stronger. It gave me a perspective on life that many people don't have."

Megan's high school years were marked by both triumph and hardship. She excelled on the field, earning a reputation as a formidable player. However, she also faced injuries that threatened to derail her budding career. Despite these setbacks, Megan's determination never wavered. She would often stay after practice, working on her skills and pushing herself to the limit. "Injuries are part of the game," she once said. "But they don't define you. How you respond to them does."

College and Professional Career

Megan's exceptional skills earned her a scholarship to the University of Portland, where she continued to shine. Her collegiate career was spectacular, but it was also marred by two ACL injuries that kept her off the field for extended periods. These injuries were devastating, but Megan's spirit remained unbroken. She used her time off the field to study the game, improving her understanding of tactics and strategy.

Her perseverance paid off when she was drafted by the Chicago Red Stars in the inaugural season of Women's Professional Soccer (WPS) in 2009. However, it was her move to the Seattle Sounders Women (now OL Reign) that marked a turning point in her career. Megan's exceptional performance on the field caught the attention of the national team selectors.

International Success and Leadership

Megan made her debut for the U.S. Women's National Team (USWNT) in 2006. Her impact was immediate, known for her agility, vision, and ability to deliver precise crosses. However, it was during the 2011 FIFA Women's World Cup that Megan truly announced herself on the world stage. Her memorable assist to Abby Wambach in the quarterfinal against Brazil is often hailed as one of the greatest moments in World Cup history. Reflecting on that game, Megan said, "It was a moment of pure instinct. I saw Abby making the run and knew I had to get the ball to her."

The USWNT went on to win the 2012 Olympic gold medal, with Megan playing a crucial role. Her leadership qualities became more apparent as she matured, both on and off the field. She was not just a player but a vocal advocate for equal pay and LGBTQ+ rights. "We have a platform, and it's our responsibility to use it for good," she often stated.

Megan's coach at the time, Pia Sundhage, spoke highly of her. "Megan has an incredible vision and ability to change the game in an instant. Her contributions go beyond the pitch; she brings a spirit and leadership that galvanizes the team."

A Remarkable Defeat and Glorious Revenge

One of the most poignant moments in Megan Rapinoe's career came during the 2016 Olympics in Rio de Janeiro. The USWNT, heavily favored to win, suffered a shocking defeat to Sweden in the quarterfinals, a game that ended in a penalty shootout. The loss was a bitter pill to swallow, especially for Megan, who was recovering from a knee injury and had been limited in her playing time. "That defeat was one of the hardest moments of my career," she later reflected. "It felt like we had let everyone down."

However, Megan and her teammates were determined to bounce back. They used the defeat as motivation, fueling their desire to reclaim their status as the best team in the world. Their chance for redemption came during the 2019 FIFA Women's World Cup in France. Megan was in peak form, her leadership and performance on the field nothing short of spectacular. During the tournament, the USWNT faced tough opponents, including a highly anticipated rematch with Sweden in the group stage. This time, the result was different. Megan led the team to a 2-0 victory, exorcising the demons of the 2016 defeat. She scored the opening goal and provided the assist for the second, her celebration a mix of relief and triumph. "We wanted to prove to everyone, and to ourselves, that we were still the best," she said.

The Road to World Cup Glory

Megan's defining moment came during the knockout

stages of the 2019 World Cup. At 34, she was one of the oldest players on the team, but her performance was nothing short of extraordinary. She scored six goals, including critical strikes in the knockout stages, and was awarded the Golden Boot and the Golden Ball as the tournament's best player.

The World Cup victory showcased Megan's incredible resilience and determination. She had faced countless challenges and a lot of criticism for speaking out on social and human rights issues. But despite all the pushback, Megan never wavered in her beliefs. "I don't shy away from a challenge," she said. "Whether it's on the field or off it, I'm always going to stand up for what I believe in."

Her teammate, Alex Morgan, described Megan's influence: "Megan is not just a teammate; she's a role model. She leads by example and motivates everyone to be their best. She's a true champion both on and off the field."

Anecdote from Teammates and Rivals
Megan Rapinoe's journey is a beacon of inspiration for young athletes. Her story teaches valuable lessons about perseverance, resilience, and the importance of staying true to oneself. Speaking to a group of young soccer players, Megan once said, "Dream big, work hard, and never let anyone tell you that you can't achieve your goals. Believe in yourself, and anything is possible."

Her coach, Jill Ellis, praised Megan's leadership, saying, "Megan is a born leader. She inspires everyone around her with her passion and dedication. She is proof that with hard work and determination, you can overcome any obstacle."

Teammates like Christen Press have often spoken about Megan's influence. "Megan is fearless. She challenges the status quo and pushes us all to be better. Her spirit is infectious."

Megan's rivals also acknowledged her exceptional abilities. Marta, the Brazilian star, once said, "Megan is a fierce competitor. You always know when she's on the field because she makes her presence felt. Playing against her is both challenging and inspiring."

Extraordinary Victories and Unyielding Spirit

One of Megan's most extraordinary victories came during the 2019 World Cup quarterfinals against France. The tension was palpable, and the stakes were high. Megan scored both goals in a 2-1 victory, showcasing not only her skill but also her ability to perform under immense pressure. Her celebration, with arms outstretched in a confident stance, became iconic. Reflecting on that match, she said, "It was one of those nights where everything clicked. We played our hearts out, and it was an incredible feeling to lead the team to victory."

Her contributions to the team's success in the tournament were lauded by her coach, Jill Ellis, who remarked, "Megan's performance was phenomenal. She rose to the occasion time and again, and her leadership was instrumental in our success."

Final Reflections and Takeaway Message

Megan Rapinoe's journey is a testament to resilience, determination, and self-belief, both on and off the field. Through the Megan Rapinoe Foundation, she champions social justice and equality, advocating for inclusion and equal opportunities. "It's important to give back," she says. Committed to inspiring the next generation, Megan continues to fight for a better world, reminding us, "Together, we can make a difference." Her story encourages young athletes to pursue their dreams, overcome challenges, and believe in the power of positive change.

Key Takeaways from Megan Rapinoe's Story:

1. Believe in Your Dream

Megan's journey started with a dream and a firm belief in her abilities. Despite obstacles, she always believed in herself. "Dream big, work hard, and never let anyone tell you that you can't achieve your goals. Believe in yourself, and anything is possible," she often said. Her self-belief drove her rise to greatness.

Takeaway: Always believe in your dreams and your potential. With self-belief, you can achieve anything.

2. Embrace Resilience

Megan faced significant setbacks, including injuries and defeats. She saw these challenges as opportunities to grow stronger. "Injuries are part of the game, but they don't define you. How you respond to them does," she said. This teaches resilience in overcoming obstacles.

Takeaway: Embrace setbacks as growth opportunities. Resilience helps you overcome challenges.

3. Stand Up for What You Believe In

Known for her advocacy for social justice and equality, Megan remained steadfast despite criticism. "I don't shy away from a challenge. Whether it's on the field or off it, I'm always going to stand up for what I believe in," she asserted. Her courage highlights the importance of advocacy and integrity.

Takeaway: Stand firm in your beliefs, even against criticism. Advocacy and integrity are vital for making a positive impact.

4. Hard Work and Dedication

Megan's success came from relentless hard work and dedication. She put in countless hours honing her skills and pushing her limits. "The more you dream, the farther you get," she believed. This underscores the importance of effort and perseverance.

Takeaway: Success is built on hard work and dedication. Keep striving to improve and achieve your goals.

5. Leadership and Team Spirit

Megan's leadership on and off the field was crucial to her team's success. She inspired her teammates with her passion and commitment. "Megan is a born leader. She inspires everyone around her with her passion and dedication," said her coach Jill Ellis. This emphasizes teamwork and positive leadership.

Takeaway: Be a leader who inspires and uplifts others. Teamwork and leadership are key to collective success.

6. Giving Back and Making a Difference

Megan uses her platform to advocate for social causes and support her community. Through her foundation, she promotes inclusion and equal opportunities. "It's important to give back," she says. Her actions remind us that success is about making a positive impact on others.

Takeaway: Use your success to give back and make a difference. True fulfillment comes from helping others.

Final Motivational Message

Megan Rapinoe's journey exemplifies the power of passion, perseverance, and self-belief. Her story teaches us to dream big, embrace resilience, stand up for our values, work hard, and give back. As she says, "You can't put a limit on anything. The more you dream, the farther you get." No matter the challenges, stay true to yourself and push forward. Dare to dream big, work tirelessly, and make a positive impact. Like Megan, you can rise above challenges and achieve greatness, creating a story that inspires others and leaves a lasting legacy.

LUKA MODRIĆ
The Playmaker of Dreams

The summer of 2018 in Russia was unforgettable for football fans around the world, but for Luka Modrić and the Croatian national team, it was a journey of a lifetime. The semi-final match against England on July 11, 2018, was a defining moment that etched Luka Modrić's name into the annals of football legend.

The atmosphere was electric as Croatia prepared to face England at the Luzhniki Stadium in Moscow. For Luka Modrić, this was more than just a game; it was the culmination of years of hard work, resilience, and an unyielding belief in his team's potential. Croatia had already surpassed expectations by reaching the semi-finals, but Luka knew this was their moment to shine.

In the days leading up to the match, Luka spoke to his teammates with quiet confidence. "We've come so far, and we've shown the world what we're capable of," he said. "But our journey isn't over yet. Let's give everything we have out there."

The whistle blew, and the match began with intensity from both sides. England struck early with a goal from Kieran Trippier, putting Croatia on the back foot. The English fans roared, sensing a potential victory. But Luka Modrić remained calm, rallying his teammates with his leadership and vision on the field.

"Luka was always composed, even when we were down," recalls teammate Ivan Rakitić. "He kept telling us to stay focused, to believe in ourselves. His presence was reassuring."

As the first half progressed, Croatia struggled to break through England's defense. However, Luka's influence began to shine. He orchestrated the midfield with precision, distributing the ball and creating opportunities. His tireless work rate and ability to maintain possession were crucial in keeping Croatia's hopes alive.

Midway through the second half, Croatia found their breakthrough. A cross from Šime Vrsaljko found Ivan Perišić, who scored a stunning equalizer. The stadium erupted, and the Croatian team was rejuvenated. Luka's eyes lit up with determination as he urged his teammates to press forward.

"Luka's energy was contagious," says Dejan Lovren. "He made us believe that we could win, that this was our time."

With the score level at 1-1, the match went into extra time. The tension was palpable, and every pass, every tackle carried immense weight. Luka Modrić continued to dominate the midfield, covering every blade of grass, dictating the tempo, and inspiring his team with his relentless drive.

In the 109th minute, Croatia's moment of glory arrived. Mario Mandžukić latched onto a header from Perišić and slotted the ball past the English goalkeeper. Croatia had taken the lead, and the realization of their impending victory began to dawn on the players and fans alike.

As the final whistle blew, Croatia had secured a historic 2-1 victory, earning their place in the World Cup final for the first time in history. The players fell to the ground in exhaustion and elation, while Luka Modrić stood tall, tears of joy streaming down his face.

"This is for all of Croatia," Luka said in the post-match interview. "We've shown the world that with heart, determination, and belief, anything is possible. This victory is for every Croatian who has supported us, for every child who dreams of achieving greatness."

An Inspirational Journey

In the small village of Modrići, Croatia, a young boy named Luka Modrić was born into a world that would test his spirit and resilience from an early age. Born on September 9, 1985, Luka's childhood was shaped by the Croatian War of Independence, a brutal conflict that left his family displaced and living as refugees. Despite the hardship, Luka's love for football provided a glimmer of hope and a path to a brighter future.

Early Life and Challenges

Luka's early years were spent in a refugee camp near the coastal town of Zadar. Life was tough, but even amid the chaos, Luka found solace in football. His grandfather, also named Luka, was his first mentor. "He was always there for me, teaching me how to kick the ball and believe in myself," Luka recalls. Tragically, his grandfather was killed in the war, an event that left a deep mark on young Luka.

Despite these adversities, Luka's passion for football only grew stronger. He would often be seen kicking a ball around the camp, honing his skills on the rocky, uneven terrain. "Football was my escape," Luka says. "It gave me a sense of normalcy and hope."

Luka's father, Stipe Modrić, recognized his son's talent and supported his passion despite the family's difficult circumstances. "From a young age, Luka showed an extraordinary love for the game," Stipe says. "I knew he had something special."

The Rise Through Youth Football

Luka's talent did not go unnoticed. He joined the local club, NK Zadar, where his technical ability and vision on the field began to shine. His coaches were amazed at how such a small and frail-looking boy could dominate the game with his skill and intelligence. "Luka had something special," says his youth coach, Tomislav Bašić. "He saw the game differently from others his age."

At the age of 16, Luka was signed by Dinamo Zagreb, one of Croatia's top clubs. However, the transition was not smooth. Initially, he was loaned out to Zrinjski Mostar in Bosnia and Herzegovina, a league known for its physicality. It was a daunting challenge for the slight midfielder, but it became a turning point in his career. "That experience toughened me up," Luka admits. "I learned to adapt and thrive in difficult conditions."

During his loan at Zrinjski Mostar, Luka faced fierce opponents and endured physical play that tested his limits. His ability to withstand and outplay more physically imposing players earned him respect and recognition. "Luka's time in Bosnia was crucial," says his former coach, Blaz Sliskovic. "He proved he could handle any challenge thrown his way."

Breakthrough and National Recognition

Luka's performances in Bosnia caught the attention of Dinamo Zagreb, and he was brought back to the club, where he quickly established himself as a key player. His ability to control the tempo of the game, combined with his vision and passing accuracy, made him indispensable. He led Dinamo to multiple league titles and domestic cups, earning recognition as the best player in the league.

His success at Dinamo Zagreb caught the eye of scouts from across Europe, and in 2008, Luka made a high-profile move to Tottenham Hotspur in the English Premier League. The transition to the physically demanding English league was challenging, but Luka's determination and skill soon won over the fans and critics. "Moving to England was a huge step," Luka says. "I had to prove myself all over again."

At Tottenham, Luka quickly became a fan favorite. His performances in midfield were instrumental in leading the team to the UEFA Champions League for the first time in the club's history. "Luka's vision and creativity were unmatched," says former Tottenham manager Harry Redknapp. "He was the heartbeat of our team."

Triumphs and Trials at Real Madrid

Luka's performances at Tottenham earned him a move to one of the biggest clubs in the world, Real Madrid, in 2012. The pressure was immense, and the expectations were sky-high. Initially, Luka struggled to adapt, and his signing was even labeled as the "worst of the season" by some Spanish media.

However, Luka's resilience and work ethic shone

through. Under the guidance of managers like Carlo Ancelotti and Zinedine Zidane, Luka became the heartbeat of Real Madrid's midfield. His ability to dictate the pace of the game, combined with his tireless work rate and creativity, made him one of the best midfielders in the world.

During his time at Real Madrid, Luka won numerous La Liga titles, Copa del Rey trophies, and most impressively, four UEFA Champions League titles. His performances on the grandest stages of European football cemented his place among the legends of the game. "Winning the Champions League was a dream come true," Luka says. "It showed that hard work and perseverance can lead to incredible achievements."

One of Luka's standout performances came in the 2018 Champions League final against Liverpool. His ability to control the midfield and his pinpoint passes were crucial in securing the victory for Real Madrid. "Luka is a magician with the ball," says teammate Sergio Ramos. "He makes everything look effortless."

International Glory and Personal Accolades

Luka's journey reached its pinnacle at the 2018 FIFA World Cup in Russia. As the captain of the Croatian national team, Luka led his country to its first-ever World Cup final. His performances throughout the tournament were nothing short of spectacular, earning him the Golden Ball award as the best player of the tournament. "Leading Croatia to the World Cup final was the proudest moment of my career," Luka reflects. "It was a testament to our team's spirit and determination."

Later that year, Luka's exceptional year was

recognized globally when he was awarded the prestigious Ballon d'Or, breaking the decade-long dominance of Lionel Messi and Cristiano Ronaldo. "This award is for all the kids out there who dream of making it," Luka said in his acceptance speech. "No matter where you come from, with hard work and belief, anything is possible."

Euro 2024: Luka Modrić's Historic Moment and Croatia's Heartbreak

At Euro 2024, Luka Modrić achieved another milestone by becoming the oldest player to score in the tournament's history. In a crucial group stage match against Italy, the 38-year-old Croatian captain scored in the 55th minute after seizing a rebound from his own saved penalty. This goal underscored his enduring skill and leadership on the field.

Despite Modrić's efforts, Croatia's hopes of advancing to the knockout stages were dashed when Italy's Mattia Zaccagni equalized in the dying seconds of stoppage time, resulting in a 1-1 draw. This late goal secured Italy's progression while leaving Croatia on the brink of elimination.

Modrić's Euro 2024 journey, possibly his last European tournament appearance, was a fitting addition to his legacy, showing that age is no barrier to talent and determination. His high-level performance against younger opponents inspired both his team and football fans, highlighting the game's beauty and unpredictability.

Overcoming Adversity: Inspirational Moments

Luka's journey has been marked by numerous

moments of adversity and triumph. One such moment came during the 2016-17 season when Real Madrid faced a tough challenge in the Champions League quarter-finals against Bayern Munich. Luka's crucial assist to Cristiano Ronaldo helped secure a vital victory, showcasing his ability to perform under pressure. "In those moments, you have to stay calm and trust your instincts," Luka says. "It's about believing in yourself and your team."

Another inspirational moment came during the 2018 World Cup semi-final against England. With Croatia trailing, Luka's leadership and relentless drive inspired his team to a comeback victory in extra time. "I told the boys at halftime that we could do it," Luka recalls. "We just had to believe and give everything on the pitch."

Legacy and Impact

Luka Modrić's career is a testament to the power of perseverance, resilience, and unwavering belief in oneself. From his humble beginnings in war-torn Croatia to the pinnacle of world football, Luka's journey is a source of inspiration for young athletes everywhere. "I want kids to know that no matter how tough life gets, you can always find a way to rise above it," Luka says.

Through his foundation, Luka has also been giving back to the community, supporting various charitable causes and helping underprivileged children pursue their dreams. "Football gave me everything, and I want to give back," Luka says with a smile.

Luka's coaches and teammates have always spoken highly of his character and leadership. "Luka is not just a great player, he's a great person," says Zinedine Zidane. "His humility and dedication are what make him special."

Final Reflections and Takeaway Message
Luka Modrić's journey from a war-torn village in Croatia to the pinnacle of world football is a story of unparalleled resilience, determination, and belief in oneself.

Key Takeaways from Luka Modrić's Story:

1. Perseverance in the Face of Adversity
Luka's early life was filled with hardships, from living in a refugee camp to losing his grandfather. Despite these challenges, he found solace and purpose in football. His ability to rise above his circumstances and continue pursuing his passion teaches us that no matter how tough life gets, we can always find a way to overcome adversity.
Takeaway: No matter how difficult your situation, keep pushing forward and find your passion to help you rise above challenges.

2. Passion and Dedication
Luka's love for football was evident from a young age. He dedicated countless hours to honing his skills, even in the most challenging environments. His unwavering passion and relentless dedication to improving his game are crucial components of his success.
Takeaway: Passion and hard work are essential. Dedicate yourself fully to what you love and strive

for continuous improvement.

3. Adaptability and Resilience

Luka faced many obstacles, including adjusting to different leagues and overcoming physical disadvantages. His ability to adapt and thrive in various conditions, such as the physically demanding Bosnian league, showcases his mental toughness and resilience.

Takeaway: Embrace change and adversity as opportunities to grow stronger. Adaptability and resilience will help you overcome any challenges.

4. Leadership and Team Spirit

As captain of the Croatian national team, Luka led by example, inspiring his teammates with determination and work ethic. His leadership during the World Cup, especially in crucial moments, underscored the importance of a positive, team-oriented attitude and leading by example.

Takeaway: Lead by example and foster a positive, team-oriented attitude. True leaders inspire others through their dedication and actions.

5. Belief in Yourself

Luka's journey was marked by doubters, but he never lost faith in himself. After winning the Ballon d'Or, he reflected, "I never stopped believing in myself, even when others doubted me. It's important to stay true to your dreams and work hard every day." His unwavering belief in his potential was key to his success.

Takeaway: Always believe in yourself and your

dreams, even when others doubt you. Self-belief is a powerful tool in achieving your goals.

6. Focus and Determination

Luka's focus on his goals and his relentless pursuit of excellence were key elements of his success. His consistent effort, combined with a clear vision of what he wanted to achieve, helped him reach the pinnacle of world football.

Takeaway: Stay focused on your goals and pursue excellence with determination. Consistent effort and a clear vision will help you achieve even the most ambitious dreams.

Final Motivational Message

Luka Modrić's story is one of resilience, hope, and the power of dreams. From a war-torn village to the world's biggest football stages, his journey inspires young athletes everywhere. "You can't put a limit on anything," Luka says. "The more you dream, the farther you get." Dream big, work hard, and never let anyone tell you otherwise. Believe in yourself, stay dedicated, and strive for excellence—like Luka, you can overcome any obstacle and turn your dreams into reality.

FABIO CANNAVARO
The Titan of Defense

I n the bustling streets of Naples, Italy, a young boy named Fabio Cannavaro found his passion for football. Born to a family that cherished the sport, Cannavaro's love for the game was clear from a very young age. His father, Pasquale, played for a local team, and Fabio would often accompany him to matches, absorbing the thrill of the game and dreaming of one day playing on the grandest stages himself.

Early Years and First Steps in Football
Fabio Cannavaro was born on September 13, 1973, in Naples. Growing up in a city known for its fervent football culture, it was almost inevitable that Fabio would fall in love with the sport. From the moment he could walk, he was kicking a ball, emulating the moves of his heroes. His early days were spent playing in the narrow streets and makeshift fields of his neighborhood, where he honed his skills and developed a tenacious playing style.

At the age of 11, Cannavaro joined the youth academy of Napoli, his hometown club. This was the first significant step in his journey toward becoming a professional footballer. Even at such a young age, Fabio showed remarkable promise. His coaches were impressed by his reading of the game, his ability to anticipate opponents' moves, and his leadership qualities. However, his path to success was not without its challenges.

Overcoming Early Setbacks

As Cannavaro progressed through the ranks, he faced numerous obstacles. One of the most daunting was his physical stature. Standing at just 5 feet 9 inches, he was often considered too short to play as a central defender, a position traditionally dominated by taller players. Yet, Cannavaro never let this deter him. Instead, he focused on leveraging his agility, timing, and extraordinary leaping ability to compensate for his height.

"I knew I wasn't the tallest, but I used it as motivation," Cannavaro once said. "I worked on my jumping, my positioning, and my ability to read the game. I wanted to prove that you don't have to be the biggest to be the best".

Rising Through the Ranks

Cannavaro's hard work paid off when he made his debut for Napoli's senior team in 1992. Despite his youth, he quickly established himself as a key player. His performances were characterized by his fearlessness, composure under pressure, and uncanny ability to snuff out attacks. It wasn't long before he caught the attention of bigger clubs.

In 1995, Cannavaro transferred to Parma, where his career truly began to take off. At Parma, he was part of a golden generation of players, including Gianluigi Buffon and Lilian Thuram. Together, they formed one of the most formidable defenses in Italian football. Under the guidance of coach Carlo Ancelotti, Cannavaro's game reached new heights.

During his time at Parma, Cannavaro won two Coppa Italia titles, a Supercoppa Italiana, and the UEFA Cup. His performances earned him admiration from teammates and opponents alike. Buffon, who played alongside Cannavaro for many years, once remarked, "Fabio was more than just a teammate; he was a brother. His passion and commitment were infectious. He had this incredible ability to make everyone around him better".

Achieving National and International Success

Cannavaro's success at the club level soon translated to the international stage. He made his debut for the Italian national team in 1997 and quickly became an integral part of the squad. His leadership qualities were evident, and he was named captain of the Azzurri in 2002.

Marcello Lippi, who coached Cannavaro during Italy's 2006 World Cup campaign, spoke highly of him: "Fabio is the epitome of a leader. His presence on the field instills confidence in the entire team. He is not just a great defender; he is a true captain".

The Bitter Defeat: Euro 2000

One of the most significant setbacks in Cannavaro's career came during the Euro 2000 final against France. Italy led the match 1-0 until the very last moments of regular time when France equalized, and subsequently won the match with a golden goal in extra time. The defeat was heartbreaking for Cannavaro and his teammates, who had come so close to lifting the trophy.

"It was a crushing defeat," Cannavaro recalled. "We were just moments away from winning, and it slipped through our fingers. But that loss only fueled my determination to succeed".

Redemption and Glory: World Cup 2006

The pinnacle of Cannavaro's career came in 2006 when he led Italy to World Cup glory in Germany. The tournament was a defining moment for Cannavaro, who put on a series of masterful defensive performances. His leadership, composure, and tactical intelligence were instrumental in Italy's success. In the final against France, Cannavaro's display was nothing short of heroic, earning him the nickname "Il Capitano" from his teammates and fans alike.

The World Cup final in Berlin was a tense and dramatic affair. After a 1-1 draw in regular and extra time, the match went to a penalty shootout. Cannavaro's calm and composed leadership was crucial during this high-pressure situation. As Fabio Grosso scored the winning penalty, Cannavaro lifted the World Cup trophy, a moment that cemented his place in football history.

Reflecting on that night, Cannavaro said, "Winning the World Cup was the realization of a dream I had since I was a child. It was a moment of immense pride, not just for me, but for all of Italy. It showed that with hard work, determination, and belief, anything is possible".

Continued Success and Leadership

Following the World Cup triumph, Cannavaro

continued to excel both at the club and international levels. He had stints with top clubs like Inter Milan, Juventus, and Real Madrid, where he won numerous titles and accolades. In 2006, he was awarded the FIFA World Player of the Year, becoming the first defender to win the award in over a decade.

Cannavaro's leadership extended beyond the pitch. He was known for his humility, professionalism, and dedication to the sport. Younger players looked up to him as a mentor and role model. His ability to inspire and lead by example was a testament to his character. Cannavaro's former coach at Real Madrid, Fabio Capello, praised his influence: "Fabio brought a level of professionalism and dedication that was unparalleled. He was always the first to arrive at training and the last to leave. His work ethic set a standard for everyone at the club".

Legacy and Inspiration

Fabio Cannavaro retired from professional football in 2011, leaving behind a legacy that few could match. His journey from the streets of Naples to the pinnacle of world football serves as an inspiration to young athletes everywhere. His story is a reminder that physical limitations can be overcome with hard work, determination, and a relentless pursuit of excellence.

Cannavaro's impact on the game continues through his coaching career and his involvement in various charitable initiatives. He remains a beloved figure in the football world, admired for his contributions both on and off the field.

In 2013, Cannavaro began his coaching career, taking charge of clubs in China and the Middle East. He also expressed a desire to one day manage the Italian national team. "Coaching Italy would be a dream come true. I want to give back to the sport that has given me so much".

Quotes and Anecdotes

Cannavaro's career is filled with memorable moments and quotes that highlight his journey. Here are a few that capture his spirit and dedication:

On Overcoming Doubts: "When people said I was too small to be a defender, it only made me work harder. I believed in my abilities and knew that with the right mindset, I could achieve anything".

On Leadership: "Being a captain is about more than just wearing an armband. It's about inspiring your team, leading by example, and never giving up, no matter how tough the situation"

On the 2006 World Cup: "The World Cup was the culmination of years of hard work and sacrifice. It was a dream come true, not just for me, but for the entire country. I'll never forget the feeling of lifting that trophy".

Anecdote from Teammates and Rivals

Gianluigi Buffon, Cannavaro's longtime teammate, once said, "Fabio was more than just a teammate; he was a brother. His passion and commitment were infectious. He had this incredible ability to make everyone around him better".

Alessandro Nesta, a fellow Italian defender, once remarked, "Talking about Fabio's height is the same as talking about the fog in Milan. I have never felt that he is short when I play with him because he can jump higher than anybody else. He is always good at heading. It doesn't make any sense talking about Cannavaro like that".

Final Reflections and Takeaway Message

Fabio Cannavaro's journey from the streets of Naples to World Cup glory is a powerful testament to the virtues of perseverance, hard work, and self-belief. His story is rich with lessons that can inspire young readers to strive for their dreams, no matter the obstacles they face.

Key Takeaways from Fabio Cannavaro's Story:

1. Cannavaro's Height: Despite being considered too short to play as a central defender, Cannavaro used his perceived limitation as motivation. He worked tirelessly on his jumping, positioning, and ability to read the game, turning his supposed weakness into a strength.
Takeaway: Identify your perceived limitations and work diligently to turn them into advantages. Your determination and effort can transform weaknesses into unique strengths.

2. Training and Preparation: Cannavaro's success was built on an unrelenting work ethic. From his early days in Napoli to his time at top clubs like Juventus and Real Madrid, he was known for being the first to arrive at training and the last to leave.
Takeaway: Consistent hard work and dedication are critical to achieving your goals. Always put in the extra effort, and remember that success often

comes to those who are willing to work the hardest.

3. Leadership and Teamwork:
Cannavaro's leadership was pivotal in Italy's 2006 World Cup triumph. He inspired his team through his actions, composure, and tactical intelligence, earning their respect and trust.
Takeaway: Being a leader is about more than titles. It's about inspiring and supporting those around you. Lead by example, show humility, and always prioritize the team's success over personal glory.

4. Resilience in the Face of Defeat:
The bitter defeat in the Euro 2000 final against France was a significant setback for Cannavaro. However, instead of letting it define him, he used the experience to fuel his determination to succeed.
Takeaway: Setbacks and failures are a part of any journey. Use them as learning experiences and motivation to push harder. Resilience and the ability to bounce back are essential for long-term success.

5. Pursuit of Excellence: Cannavaro's dedication to his craft earned him numerous accolades, including the FIFA World Player of the Year in 2006, a rare achievement for a defender.
Takeaway: Strive for excellence in everything you do. Set high standards for yourself and continually seek to improve. Recognition and success will follow those who are committed to being the best they can be.

6. Giving Back and Inspiring Others: After retiring,

Cannavaro transitioned into coaching and engaged in charitable initiatives, demonstrating his commitment to giving back to the sport and community that gave him so much.

Takeaway: Success is not just about personal achievements. It's also about how you can inspire and help others. Always look for ways to give back and make a positive impact on those around you.

Final Motivational Message

Fabio Cannavaro's story is a powerful inspiration for anyone with a dream. Whether aspiring to be an athlete, leader, or your best self, Cannavaro's principles can guide you: embrace challenges, work tirelessly, lead with humility, and learn from setbacks. Remember his words: "When people said I was too small to be a defender, it only made me work harder." Dream big, work hard, and never give up. Like Cannavaro, your journey has the potential to inspire and make a difference in the world.

NEYMAR
The Samba Dancer of Soccer

I n the vibrant city of Mogi das Cruzes, Brazil, where football was more than just a pastime, a young boy named Neymar da Silva Santos Júnior was already making waves with his exceptional talent. Born into a football-loving family, Neymar's journey was set in motion by the dreams of his father, Neymar Santos Sr., who had been a footballer himself. "Junior, remember, football is not just about talent; it's about heart," his father often told him, imparting lessons learned from his own career cut short by injury. These words became Neymar's guiding principle as he navigated the turbulent waters of football and life.

Early Beginnings and Challenges
From the moment Neymar could walk, a ball was never far from his feet. He played wherever he could, whether on the streets, in the dusty fields, or in the cramped spaces of his neighborhood. His early years were marked by financial hardship, but Neymar never let that dim his aspirations. "We didn't have much, but we had football, and that was enough for me," Neymar would later recall.

By the age of six, Neymar was already outshining kids twice his age. His father took notice and began training him with the discipline and rigor of a professional coach. His mother, Nadine, supported the family through the tough times, working multiple jobs to make ends meet. She was his first fan, always encouraging him with the words, "You can achieve anything you set your mind to, Neymar."

Neymar's talent quickly caught the attention of local teams, and by the age of seven, he joined Portuguesa Santista, a youth club known for developing young talent. But the path was not smooth. At Portuguesa, Neymar encountered older, stronger players who often tried to intimidate him. "I was small, and they would push me around," Neymar said in an interview years later. "But I learned to use my speed and skill to get around them. It made me tougher, more determined."

Rise to Prominence at Santos FC

At 11 years old, Neymar's life took a significant turn when he was scouted by Santos FC, a club with a rich history in Brazilian football. The club was home to legends like Pelé, and now they were offering Neymar a chance to follow in those illustrious footsteps. His family relocated to Santos, a decision that brought hope but also intensified the pressure on young Neymar.

At Santos FC, Neymar faced competition like never before. The youth academy was filled with talented players, all dreaming of making it to the first team. But Neymar's talent was undeniable. His coach, Zito, who had once played alongside Pelé, recognized Neymar's potential early on. "He has something special," Zito would often say. "He's fearless, and he plays with a freedom that you rarely see."

Neymar's breakthrough came at the age of 17 when

he made his debut for Santos FC's senior team. He was an instant sensation, dazzling fans with his flair, speed, and uncanny ability to find the back of the net. His first season saw him score 14 goals in 48 matches, a remarkable feat for someone so young. But success brought new challenges. The Brazilian media quickly labeled him as the next big thing, a title that came with immense expectations.

Overcoming Adversity

Despite his early success, Neymar's journey was fraught with difficulties. The physical demands of professional football began to take a toll, and injuries became a recurring issue. His slight frame was often targeted by defenders, and Neymar found himself on the receiving end of some brutal tackles. But each time he was knocked down, he got back up, driven by an unyielding desire to succeed.

In 2010, Neymar experienced one of his first major setbacks when he was left out of Brazil's World Cup squad. The decision was met with outrage from fans and pundits alike, many of whom believed Neymar had done enough to earn a spot. "It was a tough pill to swallow," Neymar admitted. "But I used it as motivation. I told myself that I would work harder, that I would be even better when the next opportunity came."

His response to this disappointment was nothing short of extraordinary. Neymar led Santos FC to their first Copa Libertadores title in nearly 50 years, scoring six goals in the tournament and earning the Best Player award. His performances drew comparisons to Pelé, who himself had led Santos to the same title decades earlier. "Neymar is a genius," Santos' coach, Muricy Ramalho, said after the final. "He's got everything it takes to be one of the greatest."

The Crushing Defeat: 2014 World Cup

The year was 2014, and the World Cup was being hosted on Brazilian soil. The entire nation's hopes were pinned on their golden boy, Neymar, who was expected to lead Brazil to glory and erase the painful memories of past World Cup disappointments. Neymar was in scintillating form, scoring four goals and carrying Brazil through the group stages and into the knockout rounds.

However, tragedy struck in the quarterfinal match against Colombia. Neymar was brutally fouled by Colombia's Juan Camilo Zúñiga, resulting in a fractured vertebra that ruled him out of the rest of the tournament. Brazil, now without their talisman, faced Germany in the semifinals. The result was catastrophic. Brazil suffered a humiliating 7-1 defeat— a loss that shocked the world and left a deep scar on the football-crazy nation.

"It was the hardest moment of my career," Neymar later reflected. "To be injured and not able to help my team, to see them suffer that way—it broke my heart." The pain of the defeat lingered, but Neymar was determined to turn this agony into a source of strength.

The Move to Barcelona and Global Stardom

Two years before the World Cup, in 2013, Neymar had made a life-changing move to Europe, signing with FC Barcelona. The transfer was one of the most talked-about in football history, and Neymar now found himself playing alongside Lionel Messi, widely regarded as the best player in the world. The transition was not without its challenges. Moving to a new country, learning a new language, and adapting to a different style of play tested Neymar both on and off the pitch.

At Barcelona, Neymar thrived under the guidance of coach Luis Enrique. "Neymar has an incredible ability to change the game," Enrique often said. "He's a player who can do the unexpected, who can win a match with a moment of brilliance." Neymar quickly became a key player for the team, forming a devastating attacking trio with Messi and Luis Suárez. Together, they led Barcelona to numerous titles, including the coveted UEFA Champions League in 2015.

The 2014-2015 season was particularly memorable, with Neymar scoring in the Champions League final against Juventus, securing Barcelona's fifth European title. His performances earned him praise from all corners of the football world. "Neymar is one of the best players I've ever faced," said Giorgio Chiellini, the Juventus defender. "He's unpredictable, and that makes him dangerous."

The Sweet Revenge: 2016 Rio Olympics

The 2016 Rio Olympics presented Neymar with an opportunity for redemption. The Olympics had a special significance for Brazil, as it was the only major international title they had never won. The pressure on Neymar was immense, as he was named the captain of the squad, tasked with leading his country to glory on home soil.

The tournament started off rocky for Brazil, with two goalless draws against South Africa and Iraq. Critics began to question Neymar's leadership and his ability to handle the pressure. But Neymar, fueled by the memory of the 2014 World Cup, dug deep and rallied his team. Brazil began to find their rhythm, and Neymar led by example, scoring crucial goals and orchestrating the team's attack.

The final was a rematch against Germany, the same team that had humiliated Brazil two years earlier. The match was tense, ending 1-1 after extra time, which meant the Olympic gold would be decided by a penalty shootout. Neymar stepped up to take the decisive fifth penalty for Brazil. The weight of a nation rested on his shoulders as he prepared to take the shot.

With nerves of steel, Neymar slotted the ball into the net, securing Brazil's first-ever Olympic gold medal in football. As the Maracanã Stadium erupted in celebration, Neymar collapsed to the ground, overcome with emotion. "This is the happiest moment of my life," Neymar said in tears during the post-match interview. "To win this gold medal, in Brazil, after everything we've been through—it's a dream come true."

His coach, Rogério Micale, praised Neymar's resilience: "Neymar carried the weight of this team and this country on his back. He showed the world what true leadership is."

Even his rivals acknowledged the significance of this victory. "Neymar was phenomenal," said German captain Julian Brandt. "He wanted this more than anyone else, and he deserved it."

The Paris Saint-Germain Chapter

In 2017, Neymar made headlines once again with a record-breaking transfer to Paris Saint-Germain (PSG). The €222 million move made him the most expensive player in history, a testament to his standing in world football. Neymar's arrival at PSG was seen as a statement of intent by the club, aiming to establish themselves as a European powerhouse.

At PSG, Neymar took on the role of the team's leader. He was no longer in Messi's shadow; this was his team, and he was determined to make history. Despite facing several injuries, Neymar continued to shine, leading PSG to multiple Ligue 1 titles and deep runs in the Champions League. His performances were often breathtaking, a reminder of why he was considered one of the best players in the world.

Neymar's time in Paris, however, was not without controversy. His flashy style of play, his off-field lifestyle, and his sometimes-divisive personality drew criticism. But Neymar remained unapologetic. "I play the way I play because I love the game," he once said. "I won't change who I am to please others."

Final Reflections and Takeaway Message

Neymar da Silva Santos Júnior's journey from the streets of Mogi das Cruzes to the pinnacle of world football is a powerful testament to the importance of resilience, determination, and self-belief. His story is filled with lessons that can inspire and guide young athletes and dreamers everywhere.

Key Takeaways from Neymar's Story:

1. Embrace Your Passion: From a young age, Neymar's love for football was undeniable. He played the game wherever he could, with whatever resources he had. His passion for football was the driving force behind his success.

Takeaway: Whatever your passion is, embrace it fully. Let it guide your actions and decisions, and it will fuel your journey.

2. Overcome Obstacles with Determination: Neymar faced numerous challenges—financial difficulties, physical injuries, and intense pressure from the public and media. Yet, he never allowed these obstacles to define him. Instead, he used them as motivation to work harder and to prove his doubters wrong.

Takeaway: In your own life, when faced with setbacks, remember that these are just stepping stones on the path to success. Your determination to overcome them will make you stronger.

3. Learn from Defeats and Come Back Stronger: The 2014 World Cup was a low point for Neymar and Brazil, marked by a devastating injury and a painful defeat. However, Neymar did not let this define his career. He used the experience to fuel his desire for redemption, ultimately leading Brazil to victory at the 2016 Rio Olympics. When life knocks you down, don't stay down. *Takeaway: Learn from your defeats and come back even stronger. Every setback is an opportunity for a comeback.*

4. Believe in Yourself: Throughout his career, Neymar has faced criticism and doubt, but he has always believed in his abilities. This self-belief is what propelled him to achieve greatness, from his early days at Santos FC to his record-breaking move to Paris Saint-Germain.

Takeaway: Believe in yourself, even when others doubt you. Your belief in your own potential is the foundation of your success.

5. Stay True to Who You Are: Neymar's style of play, characterized by flair and creativity, has often drawn criticism. But Neymar has never let this change who he is. He plays with joy, passion, and authenticity.

Takeaway: Stay true to who you are. Don't change to fit others' expectations. Your unique qualities are what make you special and will set you apart.

Final Motivational Message

Neymar's journey is a powerful reminder that greatness is not achieved overnight. It requires passion, hard work, resilience, and an unwavering belief in oneself. Whether you aspire to be an athlete, an artist, a scientist, or anything else, remember that your dreams are within reach if you are willing to put in the effort and overcome the challenges along the way.

So, to all the young dreamers out there: embrace your passion, face your obstacles head-on, learn from your setbacks, believe in your potential, and stay true to yourself. Your journey may not always be easy, but with determination and heart, you can achieve extraordinary things.

As Neymar himself once said, "The most important thing is to enjoy your life—to be happy. That's all that matters." So, chase your dreams with joy, never give up, and always strive to be the best version of yourself. The world is waiting for what only you can offer.

CONCLUSION

As you turn the final pages of *Inspiring Stories of 21st Century Soccer Stars for Kids*, take a moment to reflect on the powerful lessons embedded in the journeys of soccer's greatest legends. These stories reveal that the secret formula to success is not just about raw talent or physical ability, but a combination of perseverance, teamwork, mental strength, and the courage to face adversity.

The triumphs of icons like Lionel Messi, Cristiano Ronaldo, Carli Lloyd, and Megan Rapinoe show us that the formula for greatness is built on resilience and the relentless pursuit of improvement. These champions didn't achieve success through comfort or ease—they faced challenges head-on, learned from setbacks, and constantly pushed their limits. This is the essence of their secret formula: the ability to keep going, no matter the odds, and to emerge stronger after every challenge.

Soccer, as we've seen through the stories of these incredible athletes, is much more than a game. It's a global language that teaches us about dedication, discipline, and character. The secret formula of these champions includes not only individual brilliance but the ability to work as a team, to inspire others, and to uphold values of fair play and respect. This formula goes beyond the pitch—it shapes leaders, role models, and change-makers.

For young readers, this secret formula is your blueprint for achieving your own dreams. Whether your goal is to score the winning goal, overcome personal obstacles, or make a positive impact in your community, these stories show that success comes from dedication, hard work, and belief in yourself. It's about following the same formula these champions have mastered: passion, perseverance, and a willingness to grow from every experience.

As you move forward in your own journey, carry this secret formula with you. Let the courage and determination of these soccer legends fuel your drive toward your goals. Remember, the path to success is rarely smooth, but it is the twists and turns, the victories and the setbacks, that shape your story.

Ultimately, the secret formula isn't just about winning trophies—it's about building character, developing resilience, and creating a lasting legacy. Let the stories of these legendary soccer champions inspire you to unlock your own potential and strive for greatness, both in the game and in life. Because in soccer, as in life, the most important victories are often those that come from following your own secret formula to success.

BONUS: EXTRA STORIES

CLAIM YOUR BONUS NOW!

This exclusive bonus is **100% FREE!**

Mia Hamm, Ronaldo Nazario, Abby Wambach, and David Beckham – their incredible stories are waiting for you!

Simply enter your name and email address, and it's yours—no hassle, no catch.

It's super quick and easy!

Scan the QR Code Below or Visit:

https://brainyvolumes.com/inspiring_stories_of_soccer_star_thx/

Enjoyed the book? I'd love to hear your thoughts! **Leave an honest review** to support my work and help others discover it too!

MY NOTES & DRAWINGS

This space is yours! Use these pages to note quotes, events, or facts about your sports hero, or sketch moments that inspire you.

Made in the USA
Middletown, DE
17 November 2024

64801459R00091